LINKING OUR LIVES

Contributors

Lucie Cheng

Suellen Cheng

Judy Chu

Feelie Lee

Marjorie Lee

Susie Ling

Elaine Lou

Sucheta Mazumdar

Linking Our Lives
Chinese American Women of Los Angeles

A joint project of
Asian American Studies Center
University of California, Los Angeles
and
Chinese Historical Society of Southern California

Published by
Chinese Historical Society of Southern California
Los Angeles, California

Cover and book design by: Russell C. Leong

Cover photographs (from left to right):
Chinese American women in Los Angeles; Pearl Soo Hoo, 1912; KatherineCheung, early 1930's

Cover photographs courtesy of Lillian Wong and Katherine Cheung

Library of Congress Catalog Card Number: 84-072431

ISBN 0-930377-00-1

Published by Chinese Historical Society of Southern California, Inc.
Los Angeles, California, U.S.A.

DEDICATION
Helen Louise Lim Young

A remarkable woman whose impact extended far beyond the boundaries of her Chinese American community.

Intensely proud of her cultural heritage, Helen Young's vision and heart nonetheless could embrace Hispanic preschoolers in El Sereno, refugee students in Long Beach, and unemployed actors in Hollywood. By extending her reach far beyond her own world, she increased the visibility of the Chinese in Southern California in the most positive way. In a dozen different neighborhoods and among as many groups, she made us meet as friends, become colleagues, and work as partners.

Helen Young was a dedicated believer in the joyous celebration of Life and the advancement of mutual understanding through cultural exchanges. She was a founder and a leader: the Lotus Festival, the Dragon Boat Festival, Long Beach's Asian Pacific Art Exhibition, Los Angeles Chinatown's New Year Festival and later, its 10K Run, and Heritage Asian Pacific, Inc. With her indomitable ways and sense for good, she could remind many an official or corporate officer of the true meanings of community spirit and participation.

She was a major force, often as officer or chair, across a spectrum of the cultural activity of Southern California: Festival of the Masks, Los Angeles-Guangzhou Sister City Association, Plaza de la Raza Mexican Festival, the Dunbar Hotel and Museum in Watts, the City Bicentennial, B'Nai B'Rith's USA Bicentennial Salute, East-West Players, Council of Oriental Organizations, Monterey Park Chamber of Commerce, the San Gabriel Valley Chinese Cultural Association, and the National Conference of Festivals. She was immensely pleased with the accomplishments of the Chinese Historical Society of Southern California, in which she was a founding member and officer.

In Chinatown, the chosen community of her heritage, she worked to fulfill the needs of the people: the Alpine Recreation Center for the children, where she was involved in virtually every social and cultural program; the Teen Post for the teenagers; the Chinatown Service Center. She founded a free PAP smear clinic for women.

Her energy seemed boundless. While chairing a park event, she would prepare a feast to feed her hungry volunteers on the scene. She would cook and care for the children of Alpine when no one else could. Her creativity matched her energy. From scraps of discarded fabric would emerge the banners of a festive fairground or the memorable costumes of the performers. She was present whenever there was a need, and there was no one else. She made the time to be a wife, a mother, to be a professional, a teacher of young children.

Helen Young has taught us new meanings of involvement, commitment, and pride. She has helped to redefine the American mainstream, and in the process, enriched us all.

In appreciation of the achievements of Helen Young, Chinese American Woman, we dedicate the following pages.

CONTENTS

LIST OF ILLUSTRATIONS

Most photographs in this book are from the Southern California Chinese American Oral History Materials Collection of the Chinese Historical Society of Southern California.

PREFACE

In September 1978, the Asian American Studies Center of the University of California, Los Angeles and the Chinese Historical Society of Southern California launched an oral history project to capture the experiences of Chinese people in Southern California during the first half of the twentieth century. The joint project remains a continuing effort of the Center. We received a grant from the National Endowment for the Humanities in 1982 to index and summarize four hundred hours of recorded interviews to facilitate their use. As we interviewed individuals who lived in Southern California during the twenties and thirties, our subjects constantly told us that they were "ordinary" Chinese, who had led "ordinary" lives that could not be of interest to others. We disagree with them, because as the project advanced we became fascinated by the richness of their experiences, their struggles, disappointments, and triumphs. The project has enabled us to appreciate the extent that history grows out of the lives of "ordinary" people.

Helen Young, who promoted our Oral History Project with her usual enthusiasm and dedication, died in 1982. The Society and the Center could think of no more fitting tribute to Helen than this monograph on the history of the Chinese community in Los Angeles, of which she was a vibrant part.

A group of women at the Center decided to commit their leisure time to writing this monograph. This volume is the result of our efforts. While the Center women prepared the text, members of the Society selected the photographs. Russell Leong of the Center provided technical assistance. A joint editorial committee consisting of Lucie Cheng, Suellen Cheng and Judy Chu from the Center and Ella Yee Quan and Angela Ma Wong from the Society was responsible for completion of the entire manuscript.

This book is divided into two sections: the first is a social historical survey of Chinese women in Los Angeles from their early settlement to World War II. It is based on the United States

Census manuscripts, newspaper and magazine accounts, and personal interviews. This essay is intended to give the reader a brief introduction of the general circumstances of Chinese women during this period.

The second section consists of four papers based on the oral histories that we have collected. A list of the oral histories used in these papers is provided in the Appendices. These papers are based on the recollections of individual Chinese women and reflect the images, impressions, and views of these women. They cannot claim to be representative of all Chinese women although we hope that as a group they provide an interesting collection of typical experiences. We present them to show how Chinese women of different social backgrounds in Los Angeles during a specific time period constructed their individual and community lives.

This book would not have been possible without the support, cooperation, and encouragement of many individuals. Most of all, we are indebted to the Chinese women who agreed to be interviewed and to share their lives with us. Linking our lives with theirs, we affirm our spiritual bond and commitment to involve ourselves in all facets of Southern California life. As a celebration of human strength and community solidarity, we dedicate this volume to Helen Young and to the Chinese women of Los Angeles.

THE AUTHORS

Part One:
History

Chinese Women of Los Angeles, A Social Historical Survey

LUCIE CHENG and SUELLEN CHENG

Early Settlement

On October 22, 1859, the *Los Angeles Star* announced the arrival of the first Chinese woman in Los Angeles. The welcoming ceremony caused a great sensation in Chinatown.[1] The celebration did not last long. A month later, the woman attempted suicide. Although family squabbles were reported as the actual reason for her attempt,[2] the rough environment in which she found herself must have been a strong contributing factor. Los Angeles was a violent and undeveloped town. Its population, consisting largely of Mexicans, Indians and Yankees, was in the process of increasing from 1,601 in 1850 to 4,399 in 1860.[3] Conflicts between the new settlers and the native Mexicans led to many lynchings, robberies, and murders. It was not easy for anyone, especially a lone Chinese woman, to survive in such environment.

Demographic and Social Characteristics. Between 1860 and 1910, the Chinese community in Los Angeles, like other Chinese communities in the United States, was overwhelmingly male.

---

1. *Los Angeles Star, October* 22, 1859, p. 2.
2. *Los Angeles Star*, November 26, 1859, p. 3.
3. Judson Grenier, "From Rancho to Boomtown, the Transition Years, 1849-1889," *A Guide to Historic Places in Los Angeles County,* Chapter 2, p. 17.

Specifically, of the 234 Chinese reported in the 1870 Census, only 38, or 16%, were women. In 1880, only 4.5% of the Chinese were women. By 1910, the Chinese population had increased more than a hundredfold but the percentage of women remained very low. Table 1 gives the number and percentage of Chinese women in Los Angeles from 1860 to 1910.

**TABLE 1. Numbers and Percentages
of Chinese Women in Los Angeles, 1860-1910.**

Census year	Chinese men	Chinese women(a)	Total(b)	% of women
1860	14	2	16	12.5
1870	196	38	234	16.2
1880	1117	52	1169	4.5
1890(c)	————	——	4424	——
1900	3089	120	3209	3.7
1910	2455	147	2602	5.7

(a) Numbers recorded in manuscript censuses.

(b) Sources: 1860 manuscript census; 10th U.S. Census (1880), Vol. I, p.382; 11th U.S. Census (1890), Part I, p.451; 12th U.S. Census (1900), Vol. I, p.699; 13th U.S. Census (1910), Vol. I, p.166.

(c) 1890 Census was destroyed in a fire.

The scarcity of women was partly due to discriminatory U.S. immigration practices that barred Chinese women. Partly it was due to the sojourner mentality of early immigrant men who planned to return soon to China and saw no need to bring women with them to this new land. Chinese cultural values which frowned on women travelling around and emphasized filial responsibilities tended to keep the women at home. Uprooted by the combined effects of Western imperialism, peasant uprisings, and Punti-Hakka feuds, Chinese men went abroad to work for the survival of their families, leaving their wives at home to care for the men's parents. Should a parent die when the laborer was away, the wife was expected to perform the burial and mourning rites in his place. Even if parents were already dead, husbands usually did not bring their wives to America because the cost of the trip was prohibitive. In any event, very few Chinese families could be found in Los Angeles before the turn of the century. Only two Chinese families were listed in the 1860 Los Angeles

Census; in 1870 the number increased to 18, in 1880, 39 and in 1900, it was 59. By 1910, 61 households had at least one Chinese woman.

Due to the shortage of Chinese women, a second generation of Chinese Americans was slow to appear. For example, in 1880 there were fewer than twenty native-born Chinese American children in Los Angeles. Because of their initially small number in comparison to Chinese men, China-born females were soon outnumbered by native-born Chinese females in 1900. Of 120 Chinese women recorded in the 1900 Census, 66 were born in California or Oregon, and 54 were born in China. The trend continued, and by 1910, 99 were native born and 48 were born in China.

Nellie Y. Chung, the baby on the left, with her family in 1889.
— Courtesy of Mrs. Nellie Yee Chung

Most of the 19th century Chinese women were young. They were usually under 30, with the average age ranging from 18.5 to 24.5. These women were in high demand as wives, as is shown by the fact that over 80% of Chinese women 16 years and older were married. Table 2 shows the average age and marital status of all Chinese women in Los Angeles between 1860 and 1910.

**TABLE 2. Age and Marital Status
of Chinese Women 16 years and older in Los Angeles,
1860-1910. (a)**

Census Year	Mean Age	Marital Status	
		Single	Married
1860	18.5	0	2
1870(b)	21.7	—	—
1880	24.5	7	40
1900	24.5	16	65
1910	21.2	11	68

(a) Sources: manuscript censuses.
(b) No marital status was given in the 1870 manuscript census.

**TABLE 3. Household Status
of Chinese Women in Los Angeles, 1860-1910.**

Year	Head	Wife	Daughter	Other Kin	All Others	Total
1860	0	2	0	0	0	2
1870	4	—	1	—	—	5
1880	3	28	5	0	16	52
1900	7	48	37	1	27	120
1910	7	52	77	6	5	147

Sources: manuscript censuses.

Most of the Chinese women lived with their husbands or parents, as reflected in Table 3. Some, however, were boarders, lodgers or employees having no obvious kinship ties with the head of the household. Few women headed their own households.

From 1860 to 1910, the participation of Chinese women in the labor force grew steadily. From the 8% that were gainfully employed in 1870, the proportion increased to 15% in 1880, and then to 29% in 1900. Although more women became employed, their occupations remained constricted. In 1870, the three employed women worked as "washman" and "laborer." Out of seven workers in 1880, one each was listed as "laborer," and "servant," and two as "seamstress," and three as "cook." By 1900, more single women entered the labor force. In Los Angeles, 14 out of the 17 Chinese single women over 16 years old worked as "dressmakers," "servants," and "cooks." In contrast, only 8 out of 48 wives reported an occupation: two as "salesman" and six as "sewing women." The major occupations for Chinese women as a whole were sewing and domestic service. Of the 16 Chinese female dressmakers, 11 were single and 5 were married women who were not living with their husbands.

It was in 1910 that the trend toward greater participation in the labor force stopped. Only 4 out of 147 Chinese women were employed, listing their occupations as "family cook," "dressmaker," "interpreter," and "vegetable dealer." Many women did gainful work through subcontract such as rolling cigars, sewing, shelling shrimp and abalone, and sorting walnuts and vegetables[4] but did not report them to the census taker.

It is widely known that prostitution was prevalent in the West before the turn of the century. In Los Angeles, women from all ethnic backgrounds, although primarily Europeans, worked as prostitutes. They were usually housed in small, one-story cubicles immediately adjacent to Chinatown. Although there was not a single Chinese woman listed as "prostitute" in any 19th century Los Angeles Census, Chinese women, like their white counterparts, were also exploited in prostitution. In the early 1860's, a Chinese merchant, Mr. Chong, brought 8 "slave women" to the Los Angeles Chinatown, despite strong protests from oldtimers.[5] Although one cannot deny that Chinese prostitution did exist at the time, the extent to which Chinese women were working this trade in Los Angeles is not clear.

Limited education was a major reason why there were no Chinese women in white collar occupations. In traditional China, women were not encouraged to become literate, since education was seen as antithetical to feminine virtue. Women were socialized to be devoted helpers to their future mothers-in-law, and bearers of grandchildren for them. Before 1900, education was difficult to obtain for any Chinese, male or female. With few exceptions, only the children of the landed class received formal education. Since the largest group in the Los Angeles Chinese community came from middle peasant families of the relatively poor Sze-yup district in Guangdong (Canton), it was not common for men to have formal education, let alone women. Thus,

---

4. Nellie Yee Chung and Him Gin Quon interviews.
5. William Mason, "The Early Chinese American History," a speech delivered to the Chinese Historical Society of Southern California, April 1981.

most of the early immigrant women who came to Los Angeles had little formal education and were completely ignorant of English. According to census data, the percentage of Chinese women who were "illiterate" in English was the highest among all races in California. For example, in 1900, 73.6% of Chinese females in California could not read or write English. In 1910, the number of illiterates decreased to 35.1% for Chinese females.[6] But this was most likely due to the increasing number of children born in America.

The first Chinese women in Los Angeles lived in the block just south of the Plaza known as Negro Alley. Negro Alley was the scene of the Chinese Massacre of October 24, 1871. This tragedy resulted from a shooting between two Chinese rivals who fought over a Chinese woman. A Caucasian man, Robert Thompson, was killed accidentally when he tried to stop the shooting. To avenge the death of Thompson, a mob of about 500 Caucasians shot, hung, and stabbed nineteen Chinese, all of whom were innocent bystanders.[7] Faced with mounting racial hostility, the community turned inward and Chinese women even were confined to their own homes.

Despite the hostile environment, the Chinese community expanded from one street to the larger area next to the old Plaza. During the Los Angeles building boom in the 1880's, many Chinatown adobes and flimsy two-story wooden buildings were either razed by fire or torn down and replaced by brick buildings. By 1890, Los Angeles Chinatown took its permanent shape which was to last until the 1930's.[8] The major streets, Apablasa, Marchessault, Alameda, and Los Angeles, housed many Chinese businesses, organizations, as well as Chinese families.

Families. The early Chinese American families relied mostly on the husband's income. Because these were the only areas available to them, a majority of the Chinese men in Los Angeles found work as manual laborers in restaurants, laundries, farms, and

---

6. *1910 Census, Abstract and Supplement for California,* p. 590.

7. William Mason, "The Chinese in Los Angeles," Los Angeles County Museum of Natural History, *Museum Alliance Quarterly,* Vol. 6, No. 2, p. 16.

8. *Ibid.,* p. 17.

domestic service. Few Chinese women were married to merchants; only 3 of 18 Chinese women in 1880 were and 8 of 48 in 1900.

The lives of the few merchants' wives were quite different from those of laborers'. Merchants' wives lived in seclusion, generally upstairs from their husbands' place of business. Until they gave birth to a child, they were unlikely to be seen in public places. Some had house servants, cooks, and nurses; they did not have to perform daily household duties and usually filled their leisure time with needlework.[9] When the first Chinese theatre was built in Los Angeles Chinatown in 1888, Chinese women were seen occasionally, but were segregated on one side of the house, while men occupied the other side.[10] The only other occasions when Chinese women might be seen in public were Chinese New Years, weddings, and funerals.

This life style applied to a small percentage of the 19th century Chinese women in Southern California; the rest led much busier lives. Women married to less prosperous Chinese laborers had responsibilities as wife and mother and also as an income producer outside the home. Most were identified as "keeping house" by census takers, and were not recorded as employed. But it would be incorrect to conclude that these wives did not produce income. Many such households had boarders or lodgers and the housewife shouldered the extra workload of caring for them. Housewives of small businessmen who could not afford to hire employees often helped out in the business without pay. As was pointed out earlier, some women did piecework at home for subcontractors, but did not report these activities to the census taker.

In the Chinese American family in Los Angeles, wives tended to be much younger than their husbands. In 1880, there was an average age difference of 15.3 years; in 1900, it was 10.3 years; and in 1910, it was 14.4 years. In addition to the general tendency for men to marry younger women, there are two probable reasons for the large age difference between Chinese husband and wife:

---

9. "The Chinese Women in America," *The Land of Sunshine,* January, 1897, pp. 61-62.

10. Ervin King, "Boys' Thrills in Los Angeles of the 70's and 80's," Historical Society of Southern California, *Quarterly,* Vol. 30, No. 4, December 1948, pp. 310-311.

first, the poverty that immigrants experienced in both China and America required them to work for many years to save enough money for a wife, and second, some wives were concubines or second wives.

Tom Shee Bin, a Chinese herbalist, with his family in 1909
— Courtesy of Hazel Kwok

The typical family structure of the early Chinese Americans in Los Angeles included a husband, a wife, children and one or more lodgers. Even though large families were a deeply rooted preference of the Chinese, the size of Chinese families in Los Angeles before 1910 was small. In 1880, the average Chinese family had 1.4 children compared to 3 children in 1900, and 2.7 children in 1910. These Chinese immigrant families tended to have fewer children probably due to the instability of their economic status and the lack of adequate medical care. The late age of marriage for men may also be a contributing factor.

Generally speaking, the size of Chinese families in Los Angeles was dependent upon the socio-economic status of the family head. In 1880, there were only 2 Chinese laborers' families with children, while the other 14 families with children were headed by small businessmen. In 1900, 40 out of the 50 Chinese families living with children in the entire Southern California region were headed by small businessmen. By 1910, 90% of Chinese children were growing up in families with small businesses. These statistics confirm that Chinese laborers were economically less able to afford having children than merchants or businessmen.

Thus, not only did the early Chinese American women in Los Angeles take care of both children and lodgers at home, but they sometimes worked outside of their homes to supplement family incomes. Still the status of Chinese American women in the 19th century was a subordinate one. Traditional Chinese mores prescribed that a married woman's place was at home, attending to the needs of her husband and his family. Anti-Chinese hostility in California further prevented Chinese women from venturing outside of their homes in the Chinatown area. Living in an alien and inhospitable society led these women to cling even more to traditional ideas, and reinforced traditional attitudes and behaviors.

Successive Waves of Women Immigrants

The changes in the population of Chinese women reflect changes in American attitudes toward the Chinese and in United States foreign relations. In 1870, the California Legislature passed an anti-prostitution measure to prevent the immigration of Chinese and Japanese females unless they could provide satisfactory evidence of "correct habits and good character." The 1882 Chinese Exclusion Act allowed only wives and children of Chinese merchants to enter the United States. In 1924, Chinese Americans suffered further hardships when the court decided that Chinese wives of American citizens were not entitled to come to the United States. Due to such laws, even Chinese women born in America could not be sure of their citizenship status. For instance, before 1943, an American-born Chinese woman would lose her United States citizenship upon marriage to a person ineligible for citizenship. Alice Mar Wong, mother of Judge Delbert Wong, and many other American-born Chinese women were victims of such discriminatory laws. Born in Weaverville, California, Mrs. Wong had the right to vote and to purchase property as an American citizen before she was married. Because her husband was not an American citizen, Mrs. Wong lost her citizenship in 1924, and had to regain it after 1943 through naturalization.[11]

Ultimately, these discriminatory laws impeded the immigration of Chinese women and disrupted the lives of the Chinese families already in America. The population of women remained under 9% during this period and Chinese men in the United States were virtually condemned either to lives of forced bachelorhood, or trans-Pacific intermittent marriages.

The dramatic increase of Chinese females in the 1940s was largely due to changes in U.S. immigration policy. In 1943, Congress repealed the Chinese Exclusion Act as the United States and China became allies in World War II, and made persons of Chinese descent eligible for admission under the quota laws. A Chinese racial quota of 105 was proclaimed on February 8, 1944. The 1945 War Brides Act and the 1946 Fiancees Act also contributed to the increase in Chinese women immigrants. These two acts permitted the entry of alien spouses and minor children of those members of the United States armed forces who were citizens.

Aside from the changes in U.S. immigration policy, political and social upheavals in China encouraged more emigration. Joining the many old immigrants who had decided not to return to China were a large number of new immigrants who sought new homes in the United States. Thus, the population of Chinese women in Los Angeles almost doubled in the 1940's. By 1950, women made up almost 40% of the Chinese population in Los Angeles.[12]

As the United States and the Soviet Union competed for world leadership, liberalization of immigration policy became an ideological and political necessity. A new wave of immigrants arrived after the Refugee Relief Act of 1953 and the Refugee Escapee Act

11. Dolores Wong telephone interview, November 1, 1983.
12. In 1950, out of 8067 Chinese in Los Angeles, 3187 were women. 1950 U.S. Census, Vol. II, Part V., p. 179.

of 1957. Later during the three years between 1962 and 1965, over 15,000 Chinese refugees were permitted into the United States.[13]

Each new wave of immigrants brought more Chinese women of various backgrounds. The ones who came before 1930 were mostly from Canton. Except for a few who were of peasant origins, most were wives or daughters of merchants and the elite. After the repeal of the Chinese Exclusion Act and the enactment of the War Brides Act, more women of peasant and working class backgrounds came to join the husbands and fathers from whom they had been separated for a long time. Some female students from different parts of China came to America to pursue a modern education beginning in the 1890's, settling primarily on the East Coast. Many more students, both men and women, came during the Sino-Japanese War and World War II to study through government scholarship, missionary sponsorship, or self support. The postwar influx brought even more diversity into the Chinese population in the United States. Among them were the political refugees from China, entrepreneurs, diplomatic personnel, professors, and their families. Unlike the early immigrants, they were members of the intelligentsia and the wealthy, and were considered "elites" of Chinese society.[14] And, they came not just from Canton but from all parts of China. The Chinese immigrant population became increasingly diversified in terms of language, class and regional subculture.

The Formation of Community

After the 1880's, as a result of the Los Angeles boom its Chinese population increased while the total number of Chinese in the United States decreased. Advertisements proclaiming the good Southern California climate, the availability of choice building

---

13. Thomas Chinn, *A History of the Chinese in California: A Syllabus*, (San Francisco, Chinese Historical Society of America, 1973), p. 29.

14. Wen-Hui Chung Chen, *Chinese Socio-Cultural Patterns of the Chinese Community in Los Angeles*. Dissertation, University of Southern California, 1952, p. 45.

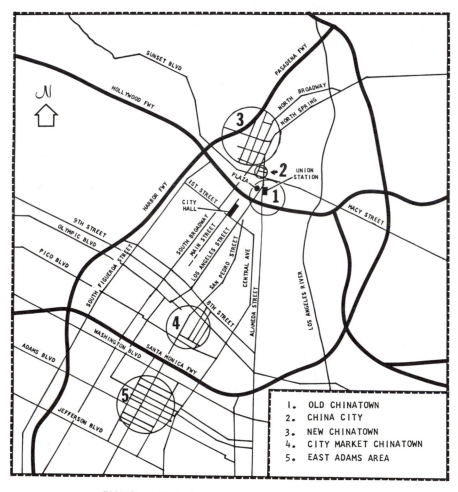

FIGURE   LOS ANGELES CHINATOWN (BEFORE 1950)

lots, and competitive railway fares brought thousands of people to the city.[15] As the general population of Los Angeles grew from nearly 11,000 in 1880 to 50,000 in 1890, the number of Chinese increased from 605 to about 1,900. The Chinese population increase in Los Angeles was due to internal migration, largely from Northern California where workers were released at the completion of the Southern Pacific railroad into Los Angeles in 1876. After the 1906 earthquake devastated San Francisco's Chinatown, more Chinese moved to Los Angeles seeking a new start.

Marchessault Street in Old Chinatown, circa 1900.
— Courtesy of Los Angeles County
Museum of Natural History

Geographic Concentrations. By the turn of the century Chinese had formed two major communities, one in Chinatown next to the Plaza, the other in the Adams Boulevard area. The Plaza area soon became the center of the Chinese community while major Los Angeles business activities were concentrated in the downtown area south of the Plaza. It was there that a two-story, brick structure, the Garnier Building was built in 1890 for Chinese commercial use. Chinatown grew gradually to cover several

15. Jean Bruce Poole, "Flow of History of El Pueblo de Los Angeles State Historic Park," October, 1980, p. 46.

blocks, with a satellite area of Chinese shops and stores located on North Spring Street to the north of the Plaza. Although Apablasa, Benjamin, Juan, Marchessault Streets, August Alley, and Ferguson Alley have long gone from the Los Angeles map, they are remembered by Chinese as well as non-Chinese oldtimers. Chinatown not only served the Chinese community, it also became a tourist town by the beginning of the century. In 1910, it had at least 15 Chinese restaurants, many Chinese gift shops, numerous grocery stores, wholesale art goods stores, doctors' offices, and Chinese organizations.[16]

In 1922, the Old Chinatown had only two paved streets and thirteen unpaved thoroughfares. It contained 184 shops, most of them consisting of one room with living quarters in the rear. Some of these business establishments operated organized vices, such as gambling houses, opium dens and brothels. Much of Chinatown was residential, with families living in back of the store or near their business location. Their first concern was to work hard and save money for the future, especially their children's education. Women's responsibilities were to take care of children at home, to help in family businesses, and to do odd jobs such as sorting produce, or sewing. There was little time for recreational activities. Visiting neighbors, relatives, or friends was the only leisure time activity for many Chinese women. Children also followed this pattern; it was not unusual for a girl or boy to come home after Chinese school and work in their parents' shop or restaurant until late. However, because the houses in this area were aging and even unsafe, many families began to move to other areas by the early 1920's.[17]

Another concentration of Chinese, almost one half of the population, lived around the East Adams area (map, p. 12) because of the convenience it offered in farming and dealing with the produce business. Farming on West Washington Boulevard and West Adams Boulevard, the Chinese grew almost all the vegetables eaten in Los Angeles during the 1880's. Chinese vegetable peddlers with horse and wagon were common street scenes at

---

16. Mason, "The Chinese in Los Angeles," p. 16.
17. Nora Sterry, "Housing Condition in Chinatown," *Journal of Applied Sociology*, Vol. 7, November-December, 1922, pp. 70-75.

the turn of the century. After 1900, however, the vegetable peddler was forced into competition with large-scale produce farming in the Imperial and San Joaquin Valleys. Refrigerated railroad cars brought large quantities of vegetables fresh from the Imperial Valley, threatening the Chinese vegetable growers. However, the Chinese met the challenge by expanding into the retail and wholesale produce industry and greatly influenced the Los Angeles produce business.[18]

In 1909, the Chinese community expanded into the Ninth Street and South San Pedro district where the City Market was founded. Louie Gwan was one of the pioneers who promoted the building of the City Market, persuading many Chinese to become shareholders and participants.[19] As their families began to move into the area, Market Chinatown grew. The neighborhood community provided housing, restaurants, grocery stores, laundries, barbershops, medical services including herbalists, recreation halls, family and district associations, Chinese schools and churches.

By the early 1920's, the Chinese community expanded again, this time into the area south of the City Market. The area extended from Main Street to Central Avenue, and from the City Market to Jefferson Boulevard. These areas largely represented the extent of Chinese residential penetration until after World War II, though some Chinese did scatter elsewhere throughout the city. For those who moved out of the Chinese community, confrontations in hostile white neighborhoods were numerous. Some could not stand the harassment they met and moved back into Chinese neighborhoods. Others challenged these discriminatory regulations and practices and won the right to stay. Generally speaking, most of the Chinese people who managed to live in restricted neighborhoods were those who enjoyed a higher financial status, including successful herbalists and businessmen. In contrast, most of the Chinese in the Adams residential area were either laborers or business people engaged in the produce business or other common Chinatown occupational pursuits. This area and the Market Chinatown reached their heyday between

---

18. Mason, "The Chinese in Los Angeles," p. 16.
19. Garding Lui, *Inside Los Angeles Chinatown*, (Los Angeles, 1948), p. 42.

the mid-30's and the mid-40's after the Chinese were forced to vacate Old Chinatown, and before the Los Angeles Chinatown of today was firmly established.

The removal of Old Chinatown to make way for Union Station in 1933 brought about significant changes to this community. Many proposals and plans for a new Chinatown were discussed between the community and the developers. Eventually, two separate developments, the new Chinatown and China City, were constructed. Both developments were completed in 1938.

China City was located on the east side of North Spring Street between Ord and Macy streets at a site formerly occupied by old Chinese stores and residences. Christine Sterling, a promoter of Olvera Street, had wanted to build a Chinese project patterned after Olvera Street. China City was created for the tourist trade and was built with the support of Mrs. Sterling, Harry Chandler of the Los Angeles Times, and other Caucasians. It was intended to depict a small Chinese village, with an atmosphere of mystery. Comprised of over two dozen small gift shops, theaters and restaurants, a rickshaw station and a joss house, China City emphasized its attraction to tourists by staging "exotic and ancient" festivities monthly. Write-ups of China City reflect the image that the society had of the Chinese at that time: "Time is required . . . to get acquainted with the loveliness and fascinating strangeness of these people"; "You'll find dozens of quaint and lovable characters in China City."[20] In its first two years, China City enjoyed much popularity and success, but its existence was brief. It opened in 1938, was destroyed by fire in early 1939, and was then rebuilt and reopened. But in 1949, another disastrous fire demolished the main section, diminishing the glamour of China City.

The project to build a new Chinatown between North Broadway and Castelar Streets (today's Hill Street), with Bernard and College Streets as its northern and southern boundaries, was led and promoted by a distinguished civic leader, Peter SooHoo, and several local Chinese businessmen. They wanted to combine Eastern beauty with Western cleanliness and orderliness in the

20. "The New China City," *The Arrowhead Magazine*, September 1940, p. 19.

*Publicity photo for "China City," a complex
designed for tourists in 1938.*

Courtesy of Ruby Louie

first Chinatown in the United States built by design and plan.
From its completion in 1938, the New Chinatown catered
primarily to tourists, and secondarily to Chinese residents. Its
new grand modern look was quite a contrast to the antiquated
look of China City. Ten years later, the New Chinatown expanded
again into the surrounding areas. By 1949 the remainder of old
Chinatown was completely torn down, and most of the Chinese
civic organizations and institutions moved to the greater new
Chinatown area. The residential area spread northward and
westward of New Chinatown, North Spring Street, and the

Adams district. The concentrated community of old Chinatown disappeared through these major moves.

Discrimination, Segregation, and Integration. The successive Chinatowns in Los Angeles indicated that Chinese preferred to settle as a group. While cultural and physical affinities provided the positive basis for group formation, white prejudice and discrimination limited any alternatives. Because they were barred from white neighborhoods, the early Chinese shared the same space with other minority working people. In Los Angeles, up until 1948, restrictive covenants were enforced despite the fact that these covenants were held unconstitutional as early as 1917 by the United States Supreme Court.[21] It was only after World War II that a few Chinese were accepted in white neighborhoods such as West Los Angeles, Hollywood, and the Los Feliz areas. Again, these Chinese families often had higher than average economic and social status.

Chinese not only lived in different sections of the city away from the whites, they were also forced to pursue different lines of work and were concentrated in the occupations that white people did not want. Chinatown businesses were about the only livelihood available to the early immigrants. Although many were able to make their way from domestic servant and manual worker to self-employed small entrepreneurs, social mobility was extremely limited. A dishwasher might become a waiter or a restaurant owner, and a produce swamper might become a produce broker or market owner, but there was virtually no opportunity for Chinese who had interests in other professions. Suffering from poor economic and educational background, the early immigrants placed strong emphasis on their children's education, hoping to prepare them for other occupational pursuits, but little opportunity opened even for them. The college educated Chinese Americans often were forced to work as cooks, waiters, or produce market workers. Jobs for Chinese women were even more limited, and were almost entirely in the low-paid service areas. Young women graduated from high school were limited to working in family businesses as waitresses, clerks, and salespersons. The difficulty in securing employment outside of Chinatown increased

21. Chen, *op. cit.*, p. 57.

during the Depression years. Chinatown businesses, relying on the prosperity of American society, were seriously affected by the Depression, and many Chinese women experienced great hardships.

Some women, discouraged by the Depression and limited access to professional jobs in the United States, went back with their husbands or families to China where trained personnel were greatly needed in the war effort against Japan. In 1932, Him Gin Quon brought a family of 12 back to China, where they farmed, returning to Los Angeles six years later.[22] Oak Yip Gee, another woman who had a similar experience recalled,

> "I went back in 1930 and didn't come back until 1938 because my (six) children were young, and things were hard in the U.S. There were no jobs, and sometimes there was hardly anything to eat. So (my husband) suggested that I take the children back to our hometown in China, and bring them back later. We waited till the economy improved before coming back."[23]

Like other working people, most Chinese were forced to be more frugal during the Depression, especially on food, clothing and housing.[24] Women would take any job available to them, whether it be sorting vegetables and fruits for the produce businessmen, or working in the canneries. Lansing Lee stated, "Yes, Chinese were affected by the Depression. But at that time everyone managed to find a job. Even if it was for $20 a month they would take it."[25] and Thomas Q. Woo recalled,

> "There wasn't enough work available. Sometimes people would look for work on farms. They would only get 30 cents for 3 hours work."[26]

---

22. Him Gin Quon interview.
23. Oak Yip Gee interview.
24. Sui Bor Quon interview.
25. Lansing Lee interview.
26. Thomas Q. Woo interview.

In such cases, every family member, male or female, young or old, worked to support the family.

When America recovered from the economic crisis, the Chinese faced keen competition in restaurants, oriental gifts, farming, produce business, and other areas of economic pursuits in which most were engaged. Many Chinese, especially the American born, felt the need for occupational expansion.

During the World War II years, many jobs were opened up to women and racial minorities. Chinese women gained opportunities to work in offices, sewing factories, war industries, and even in professional and technical positions.

It was not until the end of World War II that the Chinese gained access to other non-Chinatown occupations. The popular American image of the Chinese improved during the common war effort, as well as the labor shortage caused by the war and the incarceration of Japanese Americans. More American employers were willing to hire Chinese to work in non-traditional areas.

As the general population of the Los Angeles area increased steadily after the War, so did the local Chinese population, rising from about 5,300 in 1940 to 8,000 in 1950. Then the Chinese population jumped to 20,000 in 1960, and 40,000 in 1970. This was largely due to the dramatic increase in American-born children of second and third generations, as well as major changes in immigration laws. It also reflects an important transition made by the older immigrants, who finally gave up their long-held dream of returning to China in their old age. They began to settle down in the United States psychologically as well as physically, contributing to the growth of Chinese families in America.

The population of Chinese women also increased rapidly after World War II. In 1950 almost 40 percent of the Chinese population in Los Angeles were women. Among them were old timers and new immigrants. China-born and American-born, Cantonese and non-Cantonese, housewives and working women. Some, without any knowledge of English, came to meet their husbands, and some came as students and scholars. Certainly, the increase of the female Chinese population in Los Angeles led to an increased emphasis on family life.

Networks and Linkages

The early Chinese immigrant women lived secluded lives re-
volving around their husbands and children. Thus, American
missionaries became an important link for them to form contact
with American society. Mrs. Lau Yui was the first Chinese woman
converted in Los Angeles under Mrs. J. F. Davis, a missionary
at the Woman's Home Missionary Society of the Methodist
Church. She later entered a ministry training shool in San Francisco.[27] One of the most dedicated missionaries in Chinatown
during the early 20th century was Mrs. Emma M. Findlay, who
taught the Chinese women English, bought them the necessary
supplies for embroidery, and arranged for their children to attend
American schools. Big church weddings, which the Chinese
women loved, were introduced by Mrs. Findlay. At the first one,
the decorations alone cost $600, and it was such a success that
church weddings became "the thing."[28] Chinese newspapers
called such church weddings "Wen Ming" or "civilized" weddings.[29] Mrs. Findlay also took Chinese women shopping for
shoes and American clothes. A Chinese daughter records that:

"Mrs. Findlay took Mama to buy clothes. Her first outfit was of
plain light blue silk. Waist and skirt were separate — had lace collar,
high neck and long sleeves. Bought underwear and hat (the hat cost
$25 — with ostrich feathers extra). She hated hats — they made her
head ache. She liked the clothes, but did not know how to put
them on."[30]

---

27. *California Independent*, Vol. V, No. 21 (July 2, 1898), p. 256.

28. Louise Leung, "Chinatown's Godmother," *Los Angeles Times*
Sunday Magazine, November 10, 1940, pp. 7-8.

29. *Chung Sai Yat Po*, October 27, 1910, p. 3.

30. Jane Walden Larson, "The Social Environment and Internal
World of a Chinese-American Family as Explored through Personal
Documents," B.A. Thesis, Reed College, 1967, p. 41.

A well known and beloved figure involved in church activities in Los Angeles Chinatown was Loy Yau Chan, who visited Chinese families and attended to their needs. Around the turn of the century, Mrs. Chan's Woman Home Missionary Society for Chinese Women and Children arranged yearly church excursions to Santa Monica Beach by Pacific Electric train. In the excursion of 1902, the Chinese women and children filled an entire Pacific Electric car.[31]

Although Chinese women in Los Angeles had some links to American society, they were not widely accepted. Traditional attitudes within the Chinese community also contributed to their lack of contact with the outside. At the turn of the century, when a Chinese woman wanted to visit her friend in Chinatown, she would often leave the house very early in the morning, choose the side streets, and use an umbrella to avoid being seen.[32] Chinese parents usually objected to their daughters working in public places. By 1912, they were still not allowed to work in restaurants, Chinese or non-Chinese.[33]

Families usually did not discriminate against daughters attending schools, but if a family lacked economic resources, it was likely that the daughter would stay home and help out with family business or household chores. Those young Chinese women who were able to obtain an American education showed distinguished achievement. For example, Margaret Chung won the second prize in an oratorical contest at the University of Southern California (USC) in 1912.[34] In 1916, Nellie Wong from South Pasadena, who had worked in high school as a proofreader for a newspaper publisher, made her way to study at Wellesley College.[35] In the summer of 1932, 14 Chinese students graduated from USC, and 3 of them were women, majoring in education, music and accounting.[36] Lily SooHoo, after graduating from USC, worked

31. Mason, "The Chinese in Los Angeles," p. 20.
32. Lillian Wong interview.
33. *Chung Sai Yat Po*, September 11, 1912, p. 3.
34. *Chung Sai Yat Po*, March 10, 1910, p. 3.
35. *Chung Sai Yat Po*, October 5, 1916, p. 3.
36. *Chung Sai Yat Po*, June 8, 1932, p. 3.

for the Chinese Consulate in Los Angeles from 1933 till 1967 as a secretary, and later became the first Chinese woman consul in Los Angeles.[37]

Even though some Chinese women finished their college education, they had an extremely difficult time finding employment. Margaret Chung, the first Chinese woman to graduate from USC

Chinese American pioneer women in Southern California, honored by the Chinese Historical Society of Southern California. Seated left to right: Bessie Loo, actor's agent and actress; Louise Leung Larson, news reporter; Grace Chow, businesswoman; Lily Lum Chan, founder of the New Life Movement in Los Angeles, and Caroline Chan, schoolteacher. Standing left to right: Superior Court Judge Delbert Wong, California Secretary of State March Fong Eu, and Society President Gerald Shue.

Medical School, could not find a job in Los Angeles and went to San Francisco Chinatown.[38] In the 1920's Caroline Chan, also a graduate of USC with a secondary school teaching credential, could not find a job in teaching and went to San Francisco to become an assistant to the secretary of YWCA there. Two years

---

37. Peter SooHoo, Jr. interview.
38. Fisk University, Social Science Institute, "Orientals and Their Cultural Adjustment — Interviews, Life Histories, and Social Adjustment Experiences of Chinese and Japanese of Varying Backgrounds and Length of Residence in the United States," No. 4, 1946, p. 24.

later, she returned to Southern California, and still was not able to find a teaching job at the high school level. She was offered a position teaching English at the Ninth Street school to immigrant women, including newly-arrived Chinese women.[39] Despite racial and sexual prejudice some very determined Chinese women entered nonconventional occupations. Louise Leung Larson became Los Angeles' first woman news reporter with a Los Angeles paper. Katherine Cheung proved to the world that a Chinese woman could be an airplane pilot. Soong Yee, deserted by her husband without financial support, leased a ten acre farm and became a very successful flower farmer.[40]

In the 1930's, Chinese women started to organize themselves or join voluntary associations, marking a departure from tradition. Conscious of being excluded from the activities and fun that their white schoolmates were having in sororities, Chinese girls formed their own organizations such as the Mei Wah club.

Chinese women largely patterned their organizations after the whites, and some established linkages with white women's organizations. The Los Angeles Women's Club, formed in 1944, became a member of the Federation of Women's Clubs of Los Angeles. Its members were mostly wives of local doctors, dentists, attorneys, professors, and businessmen, and thus represented the wealthy Chinese at that time. The presidents and representatives of women's clubs in the American community were invited each year to attend the Chinese New Year tea in one of the exclusive Chinese homes.[41]

By the 1960's, many major Chinatown civic organizations and family associations began to recognize the importance of women's contributions to organizational activities and established women's auxiliaries, comprised of wives of organization members. But women's roles in these organizations were largely limited to organizing picnics and social functions and raising funds.

------

39. Chinese Historical Society of Southern California, *Gum Saan Journal*, Vol. III, No. 1, May 1979, p. 1.

40. Lui, *op. cit.*, pp. 170-171.

41. Chen, *op. cit.*, pp. 320-321.

Chinese women who worked to meet their families' financial needs did not have time to join clubs or simply were not aware of the existence of such organizations. The clubs themselves were differentiated along class lines. One club member observed: "At the (interclub) dance, the main cleavage was between the college bunch and the 'market' bunch (the latter so called because they worked in the produce markets). We didn't mix much except to dance together, but we had nothing in common."[42]

Chinese women's participation in community activities was best evidenced by the many war relief functions during the Sino-Japanese War and World War II. These war relief and fundraising efforts were in large part sponsored or organized by Chinese women. Women in the Chinese Cinema Players, the Chinese Women's New Life Movement, the Mei Wah Club, the Los Angeles Chinese Women's Club, and many others collected money, clothes, and medical supplies for China.[43] During World War II, many Chinese women had outstanding records in war bond sales. They supported the Chinese community's efforts to entertain the Chinese American servicemen who came to town by working in the canteen in Chinatown.[44] They also helped to welcome the navy, air cadets, and soldiers from China. The visit of Madame Chiang Kai-shek in 1943 brought the war relief activities to a climax.

---

42. Larson, *op. cit.*, p. 93.
43. *Chung Sai Yat Po*, December 15, 1939.
44. Chen, pp. 301-302, *Chung Sai Yat Po*, February 10, 1945.
The sources in footnotes 4, 22, 23, 24, 25, 26, 32 and 37 are from collections of the Southern California Chinese American Oral History Project, jointly sponsored by the Chinese Historical Society of Southern California and the UCLA Asian American Studies Center.

Conclusion

Since the arrival of the first Chinese woman in Los Angeles, Chinese women, like Chinese men, have gone through rough times and harsh circumstances. They sought the best opportunities they could, and worked hard to adapt to all circumstances. Although they were frustrated by the discriminatory attitude of the dominant society and the traditional values of their own community, they were able to survive and be a positive force in the social changes that took place through the decades. They made personal sacrifices for the well-being of their families, and contributed to the development of both the United States and China.

What follows is a composite portrayal of the lives that Chinese American women have experienced during the first half of this century as seen from their own perspectives.

Part Two:
A Tapestry of Oral Histories

In The Family

SUCHETA MAZUMDAR

Leaving Guangdong: Marriage Separation and Angel Island

In traditional China, marriages were family affairs arranged by
the male heads of the family; the young woman had very little
say in the matter. So when Lim Kin Yee, who had been living a
hardworking life herding the family buffalo and planting rice,
was to marry a man named Chiu, she complied, although she
had never seen him before the wedding. She placed her faith in
her relatives, saying "He is a good man." Him Gin Quon was
engaged through matchmakers when she was nine and her hus-
band-to-be was twelve. She, too, did not know him. Her sole
memory of the wedding, which took place when she was sixteen,
was that it was a grand affair since her entire village and the
neighboring village came to the wedding feast. It was unthinkable
for Chinese women of the time period not to get married, regardless of whether they were from wealthy or poor families.
As Louise Leung Larson said when talking about her mother,
"Father went back and brought mother back to the U.S. in 1902.
They were married in China through an arranged marriage . . .
Mother did not want to get married, but she knew she had to,
because every girl had to get married."

For many women, especially in the 1920's, marriage to a
Chinese immigrant in the United States meant that they had
a long wait before they could start their domestic life in Los
Angeles. Restrictive immigration laws delayed their entry to the
United States even if their husbands were citizens, and husbands

often lacked the economic means to bring over the family. Kay
Wong Gee waited three years after her marriage to join her husband, and Him Gin Quon had to wait for four years. But Lim
Kin Yee and many others like her waited nineteen years with her
son before she could come to the United States to rejoin her
husband. Sometimes economic crises forced families who had
been united to separate again, as in the case of Oak Yip Gee. She
had first come to America in 1923, but went back in 1930 with
the children, because as she remembered, "Things were hard in
the U. S., there were no jobs and sometimes there was hardly
anything to eat." She and the children stayed in China for six
years before the family could be reunited.

The family life of early immigrant women was shaped by
numerous circumstances beyond their control, beginning with
an arranged marriage to a stranger, and continuing with the struggles of surviving in a foreign land with its unfamiliar laws and
language. Such struggles often began at Angel Island, which
opened in 1910 and was the port of entry for Chinese immigrants

Women in detention at Angel Island, San Francisco Bay.
— Courtesy Reading Room, Asian American
Studies Center, UCLA

coming to the West Coast. If they were lucky and had been coached in what to say, they would be detained there for only a few weeks. If not, an error in a response could cause detention for years. Oak Yip Gee was detained for two weeks and recalled, "They locked me up as if I were in jail. They wouldn't let you out of the door, and they wouldn't let you see the outside. But after dinner, the one called 'mama' would take us all around the garden. . . . Once, just once at night. . . . We were divided up, men on one side, women on the other. . . . There was someone who had been there two whole years. Later I heard that she gave the wrong testimony and was sent back. Quite a few were sent back that way. . . . I felt very worried because I didn't know what would happen to me."

The Family in China

Most first generation immigrant families maintained regular economic and psychological ties with the kin in China. Even American-born children were aware of "Second Aunt" or "Third Brother" who lived in China, and this created a consciousness of extended relationships and responsibilities for Chinese American children.

Usually the responsibility of sending money to relatives in China was limited to those who had been born in China, but when relatives came over they were supported by the entire family which could include American-born nephews and nieces. This close association with relatives in China was most pronounced among the generation of immigrants who felt they were sojourners here, and really wanted to go back to China to retire and die. Because there were many who planned to go back, parents were concerned that their children should not become "too Americanized." If the family had enough money, they would try to send their children to China to learn the traditions. These visits to China as well as practices at home emphasized such traditional Chinese customs as serving food according to age and gender and other Confucian teachings. The hope was that the children would become "really Chinese." The contact and emotional affinity with the extended family in China made it possible for many men to go back and find brides arranged for them. And, those in China looked to their relationship with relatives in America as an important financial support system.

The Home in Los Angeles

The typical Chinese family in Chinatown in the early 20th century operated a small business, and lived on the premises. Many may have hoped for a single family home with a yard and a private garden, but the reality was much more modest. Marge Ong described, "In the early 1920's in Chinatown everybody lived at the back of the store, above the store or in buildings adjacent to other buildings." Extended family members, like brothers and cousins of the husband, often lived in the same household, making living conditions very crowded indeed. Nellie Chung once lived temporarily in a house on 14th Place, where her husband, an herbalist, also had his pharmacy. The family had a hard time finding a place because many landlords outside Chinatown would not rent to Chinese. Chung remembers, "The house on 14th Place was very small . . . five rooms and each room was very small — two bedrooms, and a dining room, a kitchen and a very small living room; it was very crowded then. Auntie, Uncle, Gladys and Stanley lived in the first bedroom, and we lived in the second bedroom." The dining room doubled as a pharmacy during the day and as a bedroom for other family members at night. Some families had to depend on the resourcefulness of their mothers who put up partitions and sewed curtains in order to acquire some semblance of private space in a congested world.

Some family homes had an altar and a kitchen niche for the worship of family ancestors; another typical feature would be the Chinese wall calendars, provided by grocers and other merchants patronized at New Year. Since these calendars were free, they inevitably turned up in every room of the house. Waste baskets and spittoons, which also were placed in every room, were used for clearing the throat, and for the shells of dried melon seeds that family and friends nibbled on at all hours of the day.

Furniture was kept to a minimum due to the shortage of space; buying a sofa which did not do double duty as a bed was an unheard luxury. Photographs of family members were not commonly displayed, for Chinese families were subject to surveillance by the immigration authorities every year; Edith Jung's sentiments were common: "We didn't want to hang photos because of the immigration officers' annual check."

The first immigrant women had been born in Southern China and grew up in villages with open spaces, trees, and streams. They must have found living in the close quarters of Chinatown a hard transition to make. But they had been brought up to be stoic and uncomplaining; they seldom revealed what they felt about personal hardships.

Family Life in Los Angeles

Mothers. The relationship of the husband and wife was determined by a different set of social values than is the American norm today. As one daughter from a wealthy and fairly Westernized family commented, "Mama claims there was no romantic love between her and Papa, and there probably was not, but there was love of a different kind, I'm sure. Maybe it was simply affection and duty, but it was a strong attachment and very harmonious" (J. Larson, *The Social Environment and Internal World of a Chinese American Family As Explored Through Personal Documents*. B. A. Thesis, Reed College, 1967). Visible demonstrations of affection were thought to be in poor taste and husbands and wives spoke to each other very little in public. A daughter, talking about her father, recalled, "(Mama) remarks that he was a thoughtful escort and always took her arm in walking, although that is not the custom of Chinese husbands. They allowed their wives to walk alone or expected them to follow, in Chinese custom. Now that I recollect it, I believe Papa was the only husband among the old Chinese who did help his wife in walking, taking her arm to escort her." This mother, and others who were married before the 1920's, certainly could have used this help, for they often had bound feet which made walking alone extremely difficult.

The lives of mothers were also bound by other restrictions and problems in communication. Since approximately half of the mothers in Los Angeles in 1900 were born in China, they carried on a life-long struggle to learn English and adapt to the many changes brought on by their marriage to an immigrant. The ease of settling into the new home depended on how well-established the husband was economically. If the husband operated a small business or restaurant, family labor was important and all members of the family lived together. The primary role of the mother was defined by her work at home. While a few of the mothers were quite educated by the standards of the time, and had even studied in Chinese schools, the majority were not educated. Typically, "mother's role was to raise the children."

Soy Wan Tong Lung with baby May, Dorothy and Joe, circa 1921.
— Courtesy of Soy Lung

The mother not only had to take care of the children, she had to help her husband in running the business in addition to doing all the household chores. Such chores included making clothes for the family, raising chickens, tending a vegetable garden, and even growing bean sprouts in the bath tub to supplement the family income. These immigrant mothers did not have leisure time to spend with their children, and the memories that the children have of their mothers naturally focus more on their roles as hard workers and as the family enforcer, who carried out the wishes of the father.

Traditional Chinese norm frowns upon women who went out of the house too much, so as one person said of her mother's generation, "Women all stayed home to be a good mother and a good wife." Nellie Chung, reminiscing about her own life, around the age of twenty-two, said: "I never went out. . . . They (the family) did not need me to go buy things. (Eldest Auntie) would ask the children to help shop for groceries . . . (It was) the same with the other women." The shopping for daily necessities was done by the husband on his way back from work, or by the eldest son after he was old enough. The seclusion of women reflected so much on the prestige of the family that when Chung's aunt went out to visit her niece Ann, who lived two blocks away, she would go at 6 A.M. so that she wouldn't be seen by people on the street. As a result of being so isolated, women from wealthy families were totally unused to travel. In one extreme case, one of the mothers went out of the house only once in her lifetime, and it took her four days to get ready to leave the house for the one-day trip. Mothers from this class spent time grooming their daughters to become good wives and mothers, teaching them to run the household, and training them in embroidery and sewing.

Not all women, however, remained so confined, and social changes in China at the beginning of the twentieth century found some faint echoes in the Chinese immigrant community. Mrs. Wing, the wife of Joe Wing, a wealthy immigrant known in the community for his Westernized ideas, was one of the very first women to appear on the streets of Chinatown. When Kang Yuwei, a famous Chinese scholar and reform movement activist, visited Los Angeles in 1905, she startled everyone by making a speech at the community reception. Mamie, one of her daughters, recalled with some pride, "(Mother) was not ashamed, not afraid to speak. She spoke on the subject of women in China for about half an hour. She said that women were persecuted and that women must learn to read and write so men wouldn't bully them. When asked if she prepared the speech, Mama said, 'Why should I prepare the speech? It was all in my stomach.' Mama talked till (she was) red in the face."

But this was atypical; most women did not have the support of the husband for such activities. These mothers, in turn, did not want their daughters to become involved in social and recreational activities that they did not understand. Some of the more tradition-bound mothers could not accept the norms of American life, which allowed daughters a far greater degree of freedom. As such, the relationship between the immigrant and American-born generations suffered from a communication gap. Many of the daughters born in the 1910's and 20's felt that their mothers did not give them enough attention or try to understand them. The feelings of these daughters are perhaps influenced by the post World War II view that parents should spend a lot of time with their school-age children and participate in recreational activities together. Instead, these immigrant parents followed a pattern common in traditional agricultural societies. The main focus of the mother-daughter relationship was for the mother to set a proper example as a Chinese wife and mother, and to make sure the older sisters carried out their responsibilities of taking care of the younger children in the family. In spite of the gaps these daughters may have felt, they were much closer to their mothers than to their fathers, and were often the ones who took care of the mothers in their old age or in sickness,

Fathers. When looking back over those early years of their lives, many women recalled "Men were the bosses in the family." Most fathers were the family disciplinarians and made the basic decisions affecting the lives of all family members. The father decided where they would live, and it was his position in the community which decided with whom the family should socialize. Even basic everyday regulations, such as what the daughters were allowed to do after school, were established by the father, and not by the mother. The father's world, however, was closed to his family even when the mother and the children were helping to run the business. As one of the women said, "Father did not believe in telling his wife and children what was going on in his life." The typical relationship between father and daughter was therefore formal, and patterned on Confucian norms of filial piety and propriety. Even in the relatively westernized Wing family, this was the case. The eldest daughter was shocked when she heard that her father was dead. "She had always looked up to him but never had a chance to really talk to her father. Chinese fathers do not sit down and talk with their children." Her father was just a traditional Chinese father who tried to do everything for his children, but his English was not fluent enough to communicate with them.

The traditional Chinese family pattern did not emphasize the father-daughter relationship and most fathers were closer to their sons with whom they could share business concerns. What little leisure time fathers had was usually not spent with the family, but with their own circle of male friends in community-oriented activities, gambling or socializing. The scope of family-oriented entertainment was limited since most wives did not go out. The Chinese language opera was one of the few occasions when the family participated together. The role of the father was, therefore, defined primarily as the family bread-winner, and by virtue of his economic position in the family had a much higher status than anyone else.

Daughters mostly remembered scenes at home concerning their fathers: "There was always a ring around the tub when papa took a bath; he didn't clean it out himself — that was too menial a job." Or, "He rarely visited the kitchen, like most American fathers do." Fathers were not involved in child-rearing, for that responsibility was clearly demarcated for the mother.

Daughters. The basic rule of behavior for girls in Chinese families was, as one of the interviewees said, "to be seen and not to be heard." This was the way they were expected to behave at home and in front of elders. They were to be even more restrained in their behavior when interacting with other members of the Chinese community. These attitudes towards girls translated into many restrictions regarding what girls could do. One of the women recalled, "Girls were not allowed to go out. It was all right for boys to go out." Girls had to have a reason to go out of the home, and they had to have parental permission before going out. Only girls from very poor families were allowed to go out on errands for their mothers; otherwise, such casual contact with the outside world was to be avoided. Parents did not think it was proper for young girls to engage in extra-curricular activities, and unlike today, taking piano lessons and other common after-school activities were frowned upon by the mothers.

Restrictions on the activities of the girls also limited the types of recreation the daughters were allowed. Many of them had to play around the house, while the brothers were given bicycles, and permitted to go ice-skating. Older brothers were often allowed to go to football games while the girls stayed home. Even though sometimes girls were allowed to go to the movies, brothers were allowed to go more often and were given more pocket-money when they went out. "As a girl," recalled an interviewee, "I was supposed to stay home and learn how to cook and sew."

The location of homes in Chinatown also imposed limitations on recreational activities for both girls and boys. Playgrounds for children located in Chinatown were not readily accessible (M. Lee, *The Recreational Interests and Participation of a Selected Group of Boys in Los Angeles, California*, Master's Thesis, USC, 1939). After the Apablasa Playground in Chinatown was closed down and the land used for commercial purposes, children had to travel to the Downey playground or the All Nations Foundation Gymnasium, which was a considerable distance away. For those who lived near Ninth Street, there was the Ninth Street playground, but for children going to both public school and Chinese language school, even that was too far away for a quick visit. Most children played in the streets. Since there was heavy traffic during the late afternoon and early evenings, this was not considered an environment safe for either boys or girls to play in though the families were probably successful only in restraining the girls.

The daily life of the girls revolved around the home, and boys were exempt from household tasks. "I had family responsibilities at home," remarked Ida Lee. "Girls washed the dishes, cleaned the house, swept the floors, and helped cook. Older brother worked at the family market. Younger brother did not have assignment chores. I was assigned to take care of younger brother, and I resented it." Marge Ong talked about the chore of washing

Marge Ong with her younger brother.
— Courtesy of Marge Ong

the diapers of younger siblings. "Mother would scrub clothing and diapers on the scrubbing board and I would stand next to my Mom on the other side of the tub and helped rinse the clothes." The older girls were expected to share the extra housework that their mothers were often forced to take on. For example, they had to do not only the laundry of their own family, but also the laundry of male unmarried relatives living with them. If the family operated a restaurant, they often did the kitchen laundry as well. Edith Jung remembers having to help her mother with the laundry of six children, the three cousins living with them, and the aprons for the restaurant help.

Taking care of younger brothers and sisters was a common experience for women growing up in the 1920's and 30's. Often the responsibility for taking care of the younger children fell to the older daughters because the mother was busy with the housework and other chores, but it was also considered to be an important aspect of a young girl's training as a future wife and mother.

In addition to taking care of younger siblings, older girls helped if the father had a small business such as a laundry, a restaurant or a grocery store. Helping father at least gave the girls, especially the older ones, a little more freedom than those who did not help in their father's business. As Marge Ong reminisced about her experience helping her father run his restaurant, "During high school, I was old enough to know my mind, and I could at least try to get a little freedom for myself. My father really appreciated my help, and did not mind."

In this case, the father let his daughter stay out a little longer than he would have otherwise. He did not insist that she come home immediately from school, making it possible for her to see her friends for a short time before going to work. Others were not so lucky and hard economic times forced them to start working for others outside the family even when they were relatively young. Thus, several women started work at fourteen or fifteen years of age as "mother's helpers" to American families.

Typically, girls born in the 1920's and 30's went much further in their education than those born in the decades before them: most at least finished high school. Many earlier immigrant women did not get beyond elementary school. Parents did not think that it was important to educate girls, and would often reserve family resources for the education of the boys. Some girls did not have the time to do schoolwork because of family responsibilities. Since there was no pressure for them to continue their education, they would leave school after a few years.

Many tradition-bound fathers, who controlled the family finances, thought like Rose Nim Tom's father; "(He) did not believe in college education for girls. . . . Believed in business for boys and the girl's place was in the home." The closely knit Chinese family structure emphasized individual sacrifices for the general care of the elderly, and the eldest daughter often had her education interrupted to take care of a sick mother.

Despite these traditional Chinese values, many mothers who did not go to school themselves, encouraged their daughters in the 1920's and 30's to learn as much as possible, for they felt that education would help in living in this country. This influenced some daughters to continue their education well beyond the high school level, and their achievements are extraordinary.

Relations With Siblings. While few details are available about the childhood relations of siblings, adult family members were expected to help each other out. Since many Chinese immigrants had only the family to rely on in times of difficulty, family relations between brothers and sisters were carefully maintained among adults. Men went into business with their brothers-in-law, and sisters helped each other in finding jobs. If a sister was widowed, very often her children would be taken care of by her brothers and sisters; many women recall being taken care of by their aunts when their own families had financial or other troubles. Brothers and sisters of both wife and husband often helped run a restaurant or family business, with all of them living together nearby.

Aunts, in particular, were often close to the family, and if mother passed away when the brothers and sisters were young, mother's eldest sister often became a *de facto* mother and took care of the entire family. While it was not common for Chinese women to remain single all their lives, some women never got married; these unmarried sisters provided much economic and emotional support for the rest of the family. In immigrant Chinese families, as in most Asian societies, the kinship structure provided the basic support system whenever possible; even second generation immigrants cherished a closely knit family structure.

Dating. Chinese American women were expected to marry young. As Ella Chung remarked, "At that time, our goals were not so defined as today, so at that time we thought we would meet our Prince Charming and get married." However, meeting "Prince Charming" was not that simple, for many Chinese American women growing up in the 1920's and 30's found they were the only Chinese their age attending a particular school. School friends were typically Caucasian, but Chinese parents did not want their children to marry non-Chinese and were very strict about whom they allowed their daughters to date. If a Chinese American woman happened to go on a date with a Caucasian, she would face the unpleasant experience of having her father rebuke the Caucasian boy, who would be told never to take the daughter out again.

Interracial marriages were generally not acceptable, for most first generation Chinese parents believed that the cultural differences could not be overcome. These attitudes seemed to vary, however, with economic class. Florence Law Hoy and Lim Kin Yee, who placed themselves in the lower-middle class, felt that their parents would rather have the children marry someone from the same racial background, but "if the young children or grand-children were in love with a Caucasian, it was okay." Others, like Him Gin Quon, who maintained close ties with their natal village in China and were economically upper-class, said that she and her husband would not be happy if the children married "for-eigners," for they felt it would "be inconvenient to talk to them and I'm afraid they will drift away."

Within the community, dating and marriage were confined to groupings of districts in China, such as Sze Yup and Sam Yup. In many cases, parents discouraged marriage outside the sub-group. When such marriages did occur, women found that they had to learn different language and customs in order to communi-cate with their husband's family. Besides these problems for young Chinese American women, many parents felt that it was not proper for their girls to go to parties or dances. This became a point of contention for the daughters, who felt that their parents did not understand their need to meet eligible men. These women recall arguments with their parents, even after they were engaged, about how often they could go out with their fiances.

Meeting the Husband. Many marriages of daughters born in the 1910's and 20's were arranged by parents, following the traditional Chinese matchmaking customs. Sometimes profes-sional matchmakers were used; at other times, mothers passed out photographs of their daughters to other mothers and acquain-tances in the community. Families often selected sons of business contacts of the father, and in such cases the daughter had little choice but agree with the decision. Some men went back to China to marry, in which case the marriage would be completely arranged by the family. None of the women, however, went to China to find husbands. Most likely, the imbalance in sex ratio contributed to both these phenomena.

Several young Chinese American women did marry men of their own choice. Many met them through Chinese social events and through the introduction of mutual friends. But by far, most women met their husbands through church sponsored activities.

Ella Ng and Fred Chung in New Chinatown, 1943.
— Courtesy of Fred Chung

In contrast to their parents' generation, those who emigrated as children believed in marriage as the natural extension of romantic love, and more than one grandmother like Florence Law Hoy said with a shy smile, "I married because of love."

Marriage and Family. Most Chinese American women got married after high school and one or two years of work, usually between the ages of nineteen to twenty-one. There were some exceptions; a few got married at younger ages, others worked several years before marriage. In the 1920's, many schools did not allow married women to continue teaching, so Chinese American teachers had to choose between giving up work after marriage, or delaying marriage. After marriage, those whose husbands owned businesses typically worked side-by-side with their mates, but much more actively than their mothers had done. Husbands in the 1930's and 40's had a more equal relationship with their wives than their fathers had had, and, though the men made the important decisions, husbands would at least discuss financial matters with their wives.

Mabel and George Lew in "Mabel's Cafe."
— Courtesy of Mabel Lew

Those women who did not have to start work immediately after marriage usually stayed home until the youngest child was ready to go to school. The second generation mother spent some free time with the children, and went with them to parks and other public places as well as to recreational events. Ida Lee described a typical day in her life in the 1930's and 40's as starting with house cleaning in the morning; taking the children to the park in the afternoon where she would meet other mothers; going home in two or three hours; making dinner; giving the baby a bath; and putting the children to bed. After the children started going to school, she went back to work, but still had to do most of the housework. "When I got home from work, I prepared dinner. Although my husband is a good cook, he came home later than I did." The tradition of housework being relegated to the women was so strong, even among second and third generation Chinese Americans, that those few men who did help around the house were regarded as "not in the true Chinese tradition."

Though many social attitudes towards women changed during these decades, many Chinese American women felt that the men in their families still had a more privileged position. In these families, things hadn't changed much and "men had a superior attitude, and women were supposed to follow." Others felt, however, that their relationship with their husband was closer than they had seen in couples of the previous generation, even if domestic work was not shared.

In most cases, the younger couple lived away, and conflict between mother-in-law and daughter-in-law was minimized. Sometimes the son-in-law went into business with the wife's family, so the woman could not be separated from her natal family. Or, if the woman had married the eldest son and the mother-in-law had died, the responsibility of raising the younger brothers and sisters of the husband would fall on the couple. Such instances were rare, but they indicated the strong emphasis on family responsibility in the traditional Chinese value system, even among those born here.

Continuity of this traditional value system can be seen most clearly in the preference for having boys rather than girls. In the first generation the preference for male children was so strong that when one mother was widowed with three small children, she gave up both daughters for adoption and kept the son. In contrast, some of the second generation interviewed said that they had no preference in gender. Still, many felt that attitudes had not changed that much between generations. As Jacqueline Gee Ung put it, "I feel Chinese still want to have sons. I don't know whether it is so much to carry on the family name or whether it is that they feel (sons) are easier to raise. Chinese fathers worry about their daughters, such as, will they get married or not. The boys, they feel, can take care of themselves." Others concurred, saying that "American born Chinese are just as eager as China-born Chinese to have sons rather than daughters."

Most of the women who married in the 1930's and 40's had small families of two or three children. Their expectations of their children changed from their mother's generation. Parental attitudes regarding the education of girls and dating had changed considerably. One woman summed up these changes by saying that in her younger years, the general ambition was for men to own their own stores, with nothing much said about the careers of women. However, in her own generation, the parents' ambition was for their children to go to college. She hoped, as had many other Chinese American parents, that her children would be doctors, scientists and lawyers, and in most cases, these ambitions included daughters as well. In the second generation, parents felt that children should have some freedom of choice "to do something that they would try to enjoy."

In general, going to Chinese language schools became less important with each succeeding generation. Most Chinese Americans did not feel tremendous pressure to learn Chinese or to socialize only with members of their own community. As further indication of relaxed mores, most of the women worked outside the home after completing their education, and some even lived on their own before marriage. This economic independence usually translated into greater freedom for the women in their own family as well as in the husband's family after marriage.

Widowhood and Divorce. Among the first generation of Chinese immigrant women, only a few had family or relatives here to whom they could turn if they were widowed. When a male cousin of the Wing family died, the young widow had to initially rely on the support of the family; fortunately, it was economically feasible for the family to provide this support. As Mamie, one of the Wing sisters remembered, "At the funeral "Yi So" almost had to be dragged away after the services in the undertaking parlor. . . . Of course she was terribly worried about her livelihood for her kids were all young. Baldwin was a baby, not a year old, I believe. It was after "Yi Go's" death that she came so much to see Mama. Then she moved next door, which was of course the best thing for her because she was so frightened of being alone."

Many others, however, did not have any family to turn to and community organizations designed to help destitute widows did not seem to exist. Kay Wong Gee, widowed with five young children and a small store on her hands, at first, felt incapable of running the store, and had to close it. As she said, "I had no choice. I was hurting . . . but if I closed the store we had nothing to eat." She could not manage the store by herself so she rented it out and took up small irregular jobs like shining shoes, tying onions and scallions into bunches, or anything at all to survive and feed her children. If widowed early, immigrant women like Kay Wong Gee, with little education and few vocational skills, had a life of struggle.

Remarriage was not a typical consideration for the first generation immigrants because of the Confucian value system to which they and their community subscribed. It was not until the 1940's and 50's that remarriage became acceptable and even widowed, socially prominent women remarried.

While divorce was not unheard of in the early 1900's, there was a great deal of stigma attached to it for women. This was even more so in the Chinese community than in the society at large. Later, attitudes on this point also have changed. Though divorce is still perceived as a negative option in the Chinese American community, there is not the same stigma attached to it.

Old Age. For most of the first generation immigrant women with children and grandchildren still located in Southern California, the traditional Chinese value of the young taking care of the old continues to operate. If they are not living there, the elderly like to go to Chinatown at least once or twice a week. Many are widowed and have come to rely on the companionship of other women like themselves. Sometimes, even if a daughter or granddaughter has a house but lives far from Chinatown, women of the older generation prefer to live near Chinatown. Kay Wong Gee, for instance, had moved out of Los Angeles and lived with her granddaughter for four years. But as she put it, "Then I wanted to come out and join the old people, so I left. She (the granddaughter) said, 'If you want to go, go, it's up to you'. . . . It was better. I had company." She and other elderly women like herself live in apartment hotels, with a room to each person, eating one meal everyday down at the Old Folks Club. Close friendships develop among these elderly women, as they go to movies, sing psalms at the church, sell raffle tickets, or play mah-jong together, compensating perhaps for a time in their youth when they were so overwhelmed with the tasks of raising a family and making ends meet that they had no time for friendships of their own.

Chinese American Women in Los Angeles at City Hall, 1938.

Traditions and Transitions

FEELIE LEE and ELAINE LOU

The lives of first and second generation Chinese American women living in Los Angeles reflected the transition between a Chinese and an emergent Chinese American way of life. Much of this transition could be captured in the changes that occurred in attitudes, beliefs, language, religion, customs and traditions as these women were challenged in their daily lives.

Much of the responsibility for transmitting culture has often been with women. In traditional China, cultural values and traditions were kept alive by those most tied to the home — the elderly, womenfolk, and in particular, mothers. Because mothers were generally the primary caretakers, occupying the emotional center of the household, they became in practice also the unofficial custodians of the culture. By their own examples and through their teachings, they insured that cultural traditions were properly transmitted to their children. Values based on Confucian ethics of respect for authority and ancestor worship, holiday celebrations, birth and marriage customs, all were transmitted and enforced by mothers. They taught their daughters, for example, to be properly obedient to their men folk — fathers, husbands, sons, and other males. Mothers also enforced customs like footbinding and bridal sales — customs that gave women little choice but were considered important and necessary to the interest of the larger society. As one 94-year-old Chinese American woman quietly reflected about life back home, "Things were bad in the old days."

However, Chinese women coming to America in the early twentieth century faced a different challenge to their role as transmitters of culture. Leaving a world of poverty, civil strife, and natural disasters, these early immigrant women went on to encounter an alien, often incomprehensible, and harsh country. Repressive immigration laws delayed their arrival, and forced some to abandon their daughters in China in the interest of sending their sons to America first. Because these laws often separated them for many years from their husbands and sons, it was not unusual for the immigrant woman to meet a stranger-husband as she disembarked from the ship. Language problems, along with discrimination practices in job, housing, and education posed further problems, adding to the adjustments they had to make.

Thus, the role of cultural transmitter took on a radically different significance for these Chinese American women. No longer could they simply transmit the culture and expect ready acceptance from their own children. Rather, their own culture inevitably had to change due to the dominant influence of American cultural practices and the strain of harsh socio-economic conditions.

In coping with this foreign culture, these women took on at least two distinct functions — that of preserver of a Chinese culture and that of creator of a new, composite Chinese American culture. As preservers of culture, they strove to maintain cultural ties between the ancestral homeland and the new home, America. As creators of an emergent Chinese American culture, they facilitated the acceptance of America as a home by modifying, sometimes eliminating, old traditions and forging new cultural practices. Between the poles of preserver and creator of culture, however, existed a variety of other cultural postures. Some women were more adamant about maintaining Chinese traditions without question, especially the early immigrant's views about a woman's proper place being in the home or the insistence on maintaining the Chinese language. Others preserved only what was possible, such as Chinese food, and family loyalties such as sending money to China. Still others adapted more readily to the new conditions, abandoning customs like arranged marriages and limited education of daughters, to take advantage of new opportunities.

The Chinese woman provided an important sense of continuity *and* identity for her children living in America. Her efforts to preserve or modify represent an assertion of "Chineseness" in a country which often threatened to engulf her identity. In this context, a Chinese mother's insistence on traditional Chinese values is more understandable. Her ritualistic enactment of customs, her adamant support of Chinese language school, or her pursuit of traditional life cycle celebrations was personal and culturally significant for her. It was a way for her to declare her Chineseness in the shifting sands of Chinese America.

Preserving a cultural heritage while simultaneously adapting to a changing world is a difficult task at best. It is made more difficult by the piecemeal transmission of culture itself. Culture up to the 1940's was largely village based and Cantonese in origin, dependent on oral transmission which is often imprecise. Since many of the early immigrants were largely uneducated, they had to rely on memory to re-enact village customs and traditions in the new setting.

Yet, cultural fragmentation was not unusual for those living in Los Angeles, given its sprawling size and the scattered presence of Chinese throughout the county. Clusters of Chinese could be found in Old and New Chinatown, while others lived in the outlying suburbs and farm areas. Some had moved from smaller towns like Fresno, Stockton, Artesia, and Hanford to the outlying areas of Los Angeles. The majority of these Chinese had to rely on their own resources, for few Chinese language schools were available to their children and few could afford to hire tutors. Transportation was limited and traditional attitudes regarding a woman's domestic role combined to contribute to their isolation.

While Chinese American women attempted to retain elements of the culture, they were simultaneously forging new, even hybrid forms. In adapting to the changed environment, these women embodied the transitions from a Chinese to a Chinese American way of life. The cultural transitions was more difficult on the whole with the early immigrant women, whose language problems and social isolation prevented an easy adaptation. However, their daughters and granddaughters, children of Chinese America, acculturated more easily, instead facing a different problem — the retention of a rapidly eroding Chinese cultural life. Which cul-

tural elements, then, did these women manage to preserve and
which did they modify or eliminate while living in Los Angeles
during the first half of this century?

Language

In the transition of cultures, the Chinese language suffered the
most erosion as English rapidly became the first language, especially with second and third generation women. The loss of
Chinese with the corresponding gain of English signaled the
emergence of a Chinese American way of life. Certainly, language
is an index of culture and communication. A person's acceptance
of and by a society relates directly to one's language proficiency
in, in this case, English. "No matter what, I'm still Chinese because I don't understand English . . . and when whites talk to me,
I can't understand," one Chinese woman stated. For many of
these first generation Chinese women, embracing English and
thereby American culture was secondary to retaining their own
native Chinese. The minimal education most immigrant women
had and their difficulty in learning a new language in their 20's
and 30's also contributed to their lack of facility to speak English.
Moreover, the geographical sprawl of Los Angeles and the few
available or accessible English language schools exacerbated an
already difficult situation for the early immigrants in learning
English and for their daughters to maintain proficiency in Chinese. Adult education classes in cultural adjustment and English
were offered in some junior high and elementary schools, but
were not readily available to working couples, let alone accessible to the majority, without transportation in the early years.
Churches were among the few places which offered English lessons as well as cultural adjustment classes. Thus, one woman
admitted that she went to Bible School in order to learn English
rather than to worship. The Caucasian missionaries who sometimes sponsored Chinese brides furthered their acculturation
through class sessions.

These women maintained pride in their culture and identity
through Chinese language and cultural education, saying, "I

wanted my children to know about the culture and civilization of their homeland." To them, China was still the homeland, and a place to which they might one day return. Mothers feared that without fluency in Chinese, their children would not be able to function in China nor would they be able to maintain ties with those remaining relatives. "I'd like him to study Chinese and also to study English; always both, otherwise, when people back home (China) send letters he won't be able to read them. The people at home don't know English . . ." One mother resorted to incentives in an effort to encourage her children: "I would give them anything they wanted as long as they asked me in Chinese."

In some homes, the importance of a Chinese education was so great that it justified sending a child to China or Hong Kong to receive several years of proper Chinese education. As one woman said, "To send children back to China is to instill them with Chinese culture for a balanced life." The need for such an education produced a number of schools in Los Angeles that taught language and culture in the Cantonese dialect. In spite of their limited funds, families often struggled to send their children to

Many Chinese Americans were sent to Chinese school as well as to American school; this Chinese school class photograph was taken in 1933 in Old Chinatown.
— Courtesy of Marge and Oliver Ong

these schools. But there were only a few such schools in existence. Thus, some had to hire a tutor or had to have a willing cousin to assume the task of teaching the children at home.

Chinese school was considered a "social thing" by many students who attended. Usually located in Chinatown, it was a place to congregate and find companionship and solace with peers of similar race, culture and background. This was especially the case for those who attended predominantly white schools where the environment there might be less than friendly, if not hostile. Nonetheless, three hours of Chinese each day after a full session in regular school was a considerable strain. Those less than enthusiastic about their experience in Chinese school remarked, "Chinese school was a drag," or, "When my Chinese school was torn down, it was the happiest day in my life."

Yet these same Chinese women often expressed profound regret for not having kept up with their Chinese. "I regret everyday that I didn't learn Chinese . . . I see all the things I missed, like being able to talk to my father." They were even more sorry about their own children who showed even less interest in Chinese. Recognizing the futility of forcing Chinese on their own children or grandchildren, many allowed the inevitable to occur. On the other hand, there were women who had not retained any of their Chinese and found little need or opportunity for it in their lives. These women generally lived and worked among Caucasians and considered themselves "more American than Chinese."

Although very few second and third generation children were able to maintain fluency in Chinese, those who did appeared to have great pride in their bilingual/bicultural status: "I am grateful for the Chinese culture because I can understand both cultures. I believe Chinese culture is best."

Religion

Traditional religion in China was a mixture of Buddhism, Confucianism and Taoism, presenting a more philosophical outlook on life than the more institutionalized moral order found in the West. The co-existence of these "religions" was partially reinforced by the political turmoil throughout China's history which denied any one religion a permanent or official status. This undoubtedly made it easier for the early immigrant Chinese women to accommodate to Western religion while simultaneously maintaining their Chinese gods. Though some of the women describe themselves as primarily Catholic, many were Protestant i.e., Presbyterian, Methodist, Baptist, and Congregational. Even with this kind of identification, it was common to find in their homes an altar for ancestor worship alongside a Bible and crucifix. Incense would burn on certain days and on annual visits at the gravesites (Ching Ming) with the accompanying food and ritual observances preserved, even if the burial ceremonies were Western oriented. Moreover, it was not unusual to find women attending Kong Chow Temple on Ferguson Alley in Old Chinatown while simultaneously declaring themselves Christians.

Kong Chow Temple was established just before the turn of the century, not long after the first Chinese temple was built in San Francisco. Built by and for the people from Sun Wui and Hok Sahn district of Guangdong, it served as a religious, cultural, and social center. Visits to the temple were especially important at the beginning of New Year to seek blessings from the gods and to have fortunes told. While many of the women spoke about their Protestant affiliations and church weddings, they also recalled burning incense before a family altar, praying in the temple, or acknowledging the Chinese gods that watched over their home. Religious observances were marked by the Chinese lunar calendar even though the Western calendar had been adopted. Images of Kuan Ti, the God of War, were found in many Chinese American homes.

American churches fulfilled many functions for the Chinese immigrant woman. A fundamental introduction to American life and culture, the churches provided educational and cultural services for the woman, as well as activities for their children. English and American customs were taught through the efforts of missionaries like Emma Findlay. Adult English and cultural-adjustment classes were offered through local schools that were affiliated with the churches of Chinatown. Activities for children were coordinated by the church, enabling them to experience a world beyond Chinatown. "Without the Chinese Catholic Center, I would not have been able to participate in activities outside of Chinatown." Mountain trips, plays, summer school, or fishing were a luxury to children whose parents seldom had the time or money to indulge in recreational outings or vacations. Some churches formed teams for sports such as basketball, which sparked the interest of many children.

The church was an important social outlet for many of the women, who were largely excluded from essentially male-dominated family associations. It became a place for women to meet their future husband and, in fact, the church was increasingly the socially acceptable place in which "modern" marriages could take place. However, once married, women found less time to attend church. It was not until their advanced years that some women returned to the church for solace, comfort, and companionship.

Religion per se was not a dominant force in the lives of these women. Rather, these Western institutions provided a social outlet combined with the selective observance of certain Chinese religious traditions. As subsequent generations of American-born Chinese appeared, however, these traditions became a part of history, sometimes practiced without comprehension.

Holidays, Festivals and Celebrations

Holidays and festivals often contained religious and social elements. Traditional Chinese holidays promoted social gatherings while celebrating religious traditions like ancestor worship. Women were usually responsible for preparing the dishes around which the festivities centered. Chinese New Year was the most commonly celebrated holiday with women preparing special dishes such as "jaai" (a vegetable dish) and dried oysters. Customs like housecleaning, paying off debts, and offering money wrapped in red paper to children often accompanied the onset of the New Year. First generation women observed the social edict that they were to venture only into the streets on New Year's night with their faces covered by a fan or umbrella.

On other holidays also, specially-made food and certain fruits and condiments invariably accompanied the observances. For example, during the Dragon Boat Festival, the fifth day of the fifth month which commemorates a Chinese scholar who drowned himself, women spent long hours tediously preparing Chinese "tamales" made of sticky rice wrapped in bamboo leaves. These were shared with friends and relatives. Moon cakes, a heavy, round, bean pastry used to celebrate the Mid-Autumn Festival, were no longer made at home by these women, but easily purchased from the local Chinese grocer. The importance of other traditional Chinese holidays like Ching Ming, Harvest Festival, Buddha's birthday, however, diminished with time and acculturation. Eventually, Western holidays, like Christmas and Thanksgiving, became a more dominant part of the Chinese American way of life.

The life cycle of birth, marriage, and death were still celebrated with modifications. Many continued the custom of "Moon-yuet," the one month old celebration of a baby's birth with a hair cutting ritual, red eggs and ginger, and accompanying banquet. Early

A church wedding.
— Courtesy of Marge and Oliver Ong

immigrant women recalled the more joyous celebration of a son's birth over a daughter's, but eventually the fact that children were born at all, overshadowed the differences between a son's or a daughter's birth celebration.

The celebration of marriage took on increasingly Western aspects. Unlike traditional weddings in China which lasted four to seven days complete with sedan chairs, phoenix crowns, and an abundance of food, marriage ceremonies typically took place in a Western church followed by a Chinese banquet and an American honeymoon. It became fashionable to have a church wedding, which was a sign of a modern Chinese American couple.

A Chinese-style wedding banquet.
— Courtesy of Grace Chow

Funerals underwent substantial changes, given the new setting and the difficulty of garnering the necessary monies for a full ceremonial display. However, elements of traditional funeral observances were retained, such as the parade through town with the marching band, the funeral procession which passed the house of the deceased, the funeral banquet, and the candy shared with guests. Coins were sometimes distributed among the attendees to spread the Sa Hee or polluted air associated with death so that it might evaporate.

In these holiday and life-cycle celebrations women played an important role in the preparation and enactment of old traditions in the new setting. Immigrant women understandably were more familiar with the rituals than their American-born daughters. Their observances of such traditions, then, became one of the last links of an increasingly tenuous hold with the ancestral homeland.

Recreation

First generation Chinese women rarely had much opportunity for leisure because they worked long hours at home or in family businesses. Language barriers, unfamiliarity with Western culture, social isolation, and racial discrimination further limited their options for recreation. Their major concern was survival of the family and the expectation that their children would have an easier life.

What spare time available was spent at the Chinese movies, opera, or theater. Those more indulgent might venture to the racetracks or, after World War II, to the "Gambling City" of Las Vegas. Mah jong, a popular game for many women, served primarily as a social event although it was also financially helpful to the winners. "I usually play about once a week for about five to six hours." Even though some Christian women regarded the game disfavorably because they equated it with gambling, it was, according to one woman, "Not always gambling. The money goes in a jackpot and afterwards there's dinner and dancing for all."

With succeeding generations of Chinese women, recreational activities increased as economic stability became more assured. As more worked outside the home, formerly binding social dictates and family responsibilities gave way gradually and leisure time activities became more possible. American-born Chinese women understandably showed less interest in Chinese operas, movies, or traditional festivities because they had difficulty understanding them. Instead, they seemed to prefer American forms of entertainment, like movies, picnics, and sports. They took pleasure in games like tennis, basketball, swimming, baseball, skating, and dancing — activities previously unheard of for Chinese women in the early years of immigration.

In fact, as leisure time became more affordable and acculturation made its mark, a major entertainment event like the Miss Chinatown Pageant became a community focal point. Held nationally since the early 1960's, and locally since the 1970's, the Pageant is a prime example of the blending of Chinese and American values. Sponsored by the Chinese Chamber of Commerce of Los Angeles, it is one of the most widely attended and most popular Chinese events each year. Girls between the ages of 18-24 are selected on the basis of poise, appearance, personality, facial and physical appearance. According to one coordinator of the event, the Pageant encourages "young Chinese girls to participate in Chinese events to build their interest in the Chinese community and develop more knowledge of their cultural background and self-confidence and presenting themselves to the public." Like American beauty pageants, Chinese girls appear in Western bathing suits and Chinese dresses, the cheong sam. The judges often include Caucasians as well as Chinese while the contestants include women of full or partial Chinese extraction.

The Pageant is a far cry from traditional Chinese customs which just forty years earlier stressed modesty and deference in women, and discouraged them from showing their faces in public, let alone their bodies. It appears that the appeal of the contest is not to glorify Chinese culture and virtues, but to present them in a manner comparable to their American counterparts.

Food

Amid all the cultural permutations that occurred with Chinese language, social customs, and traditions, Chinese food remained relatively unchanged. Its preparation, ingredients, service, and cultural significance remained distinctively Chinese. Although these women prepared Western dishes, savored "homemade ice cream and watermelon," or adopted foods associated with Thanksgiving and Christmas, such foods were no substitute for Chinese cooking. Moreover, Chinese cooking techniques were often used to prepare American food, such as stir frying meat and vegetables or preparing chop suey — the mixed miscellany of Cantonese cooking using both Western and Chinese ingredients. Even those second or third generation women who did not know how to cook Chinese food preferred eating it. Rice, a traditional staple in South China is served at least once a day. One woman even taught her Mexican neighbor how to cook rice Chinese style, thereby initiating a friendship which lasted for decades.

Food provided the common link among these women, since they had the responsibility of cooking and serving. Food became one of the chief means, then, for women, to reaffirm an important element of Chinese culture.

Food embodies many levels of meaning in Chinese culture — and is amply reflected in the Los Angeles women's response to it. Food is a central, organizing force in the life of one 74-year-old Cantonese woman: taro cakes, restaurant eating, and the pleasure associated with a full stomach punctuate her interview. Being well-fed by her children is equated with security and happiness: "Now I have no cares and worries. I go to church all day. I'm very happy. They (children) feed me all day." At the end of the interview her joyful anticipation of her visiting her daughter is associated with their eating together. It appears that food is not the only culturally significant but also a sign of emotional well-being.

Chinese food was also intimately connected with social customs that ranged from the token gift of food that guests brought their hosts to the special dim sum dishes prepared at home to the sumptuous banquets that accompanied holidays and life cycle celebrations. One grandmother arduously ground her flour from rice to make rice cakes and dim sum, some of which were delivered to the clan association and to the residences of bachelors. Special foods like moon cakes, "joongs" (sweet rice mixture wrapped in bamboo leaves), or "fat choy" (hair vegetables) were prepared during certain holiday celebrations, such as New Year, Mid-Autumn and the Spring Festivals. Each type of food carried a special meaning. For instance, the preparation of hair vegetables signified hope for wealth since the sounds for "fat choy" were identical with those for "becoming wealthy" in Cantonese. Such festival dishes could be found in the homes of second and third generation Chinese even though these were often bought rather than prepared at home. It was not uncommon for many immigrant women to prepare special foods as they performed the rites of ancestor worship. Many women recalled the offerings of chicken, pork, rice, and wine placed in front of the family altar.

Chinese food not only provided a link to a cultural tradition, but also proved to be a social catalyst. The arrival of a new baby would be an occasion for two generations of women from aunts to grandmothers to gather in the kitchen. Clan dinners and holiday banquets brought friends and relatives together to socialize and celebrate after working an arduous six to seven-day week. Such banquet occasions also introduced Americans to Chinese traditions, facilitating greater communications with the non-Chinese world.

Those women who valued herbal as well as Western medicine also freely used certain Chinese herbs in their food preparation, and were often willing to pay high prices in order to prepare the desired dishes correctly. The medicinal properties of certain soups and broths were important to certain customs. Chicken soup laced with Chinese whiskey was given to mothers during the post-partum period; picked pigs feet were prepared at the birth of a baby; red eggs and ginger accompanied the month-old child's hair cutting celebration; and pieces of candy were distributed to funeral guests to sweeten the bitterness of death. These very traditions continue today even though not everyone practices nor understands them.

The complexity of Chinese cuisine reflects, in many ways, the Chinese culture itself: an intricate and complex mixture of ingredients cut into particular sizes and shapes, cooked in various styles with flavors harmonized according to certain rules. Moreover, it is highly regionalized with its own orthodoxy of preparation and often steeped in history and tradition. With its medicinal properties, its philosophical underpinnings, its socio-cultural and religious significance, Chinese food remains one of the chief means by which these Chinese American women transmitted and adapted their culture.

Chinese American women honored for their achievements at California State University, Los Angeles, 1984. Seated left-to-right: Bessie Loo, arts; Maye Wong, community; Lily Lum Chan, community; Mrs. Him Gin Quon, community. Standing left-to-right: Lily Lee Chen, politics; Annie Chin Siu, dentistry; Dolores Wong, community; Louise Leung Larson, journalism; and Lilly Mu Lee, business and community.
— Photo Courtesy of California State University, Los Angeles

Chinese Women at Work

JUDY CHU and SUSIE LING

Introduction

The Chinese immigrant woman at the turn of the century was usually expected to be working solely in the household taking care of the family. In the 1920's and 30's, however, the Chinese American family found it increasingly acceptable and necessary for a daughter or a mother to become wage earners or work in the family business. This trend continued into the 1940's when Chinese American women worked for the war effort. It was not until the 1950's that more Chinese American women were able to pursue careers.

These women helped substantially the economic survival of the Chinese, but their contributions were rarely recognized by either their families or themselves. Many of them, with little fanfare, worked to help the family in a succession of jobs as clerks, secretaries, cashiers and other occupations. They coped with discriminatory practices, worked long and hard hours, and took care of family duties all at the same time.

This life of invisibility was in keeping with the values of the traditional Chinese immigrant at the turn of the century. Daughters were taught to be "seen but not heard"; they were to be obedient and not too active and aggressive. Their proper place was in the home rather than at school or at a job. Such admonitions shaped these Chinese American women's view of themselves in the decades to come. It took an unusual woman to pursue a career before fulfilling the responsibilities of marriage and children.

But the hard times of the 1920's and 30's necessitated that Chinese women contribute to the family income in a variety of ways. A few pursued jobs; more often, they were unpaid laborers in the home or in family business. Most typically, they were housewives. As the mainstays of the family, they ran the household and even the finances, taking every opportunity to contribute to the family income. They organized household members to crack or sort walnuts or to address envelopes for a little extra money, since every penny counted.

If there was a restaurant, store or laundry, there was no question that it was the filial duty of both women and children to work in such businesses, paid or not. However, it was in this setting that these women sometimes gained substantial training in business management. Taking major responsibilities for the businesses, they were the accountants or clerks, and in some cases, the "bosses" when their husbands fell ill or returned to China.

A few young Chinese American women in the 1920's and 30's tried to work for wages in the non-Chinese world as clerks, secretaries, garment workers, teachers and other occupations. But the heightened discrimination of that period made working in such jobs difficult. One female clerk recalls, "In the 20's, we were always behind the scenes. They didn't trust us in the sales department. They didn't hire Chinese girls until the 40's. We just dusted the place and did cashiering. In those days, minorities just weren't given good jobs." This kind of discrimination, on top of competing family responsibilities, led to a situation in which Chinese American women went from job to job, thus precluding the development of a career.

Chinese American women did not make a substantial foray into mainstream jobs until the 40's when women were called upon to work due to the absence of men during the war. Not only were Chinese American women hired as clerks and secretaries, but a few became "Rosie the Riveters," that is, women who worked as welders and riveters at defense plants during the war.

A small number of mainstream jobs were also attained by Chinese American parents of the 1920's and 30's who dreamed that the second generation would become successful professionals in America. Even though they mainly put such pressure on sons, a few families also saw the value in educating a highly aspiring daughter. As a result, there were some Chinese American women who pursued undergraduate and graduate degrees at places like the University of Southern California and the University of California at Los Angeles in the 1920's and 30's. There were few Chinese students, let alone female Chinese students attending then. While reaction to them, on the whole, was fair, some remember vividly the racial remarks that were made, such as one teacher saying, "All foreigners should stay in their country."

Nevertheless, education spawned the first Chinese American women professionals in the 1930's and 40's. Among their ranks are journalists, real estate investors, insurance agents, actresses, nurses, social workers, and teachers. More often than not, they "happened" upon their careers. In some cases, discrimination barred these women from getting the job for which they were educated, and they ended up in other occupations. For others, hardship circumstances such as family illnesses, divorce or economic problems were the impetus to seeking a career. Still others pursued careers because they wanted to use their professional skills to go back and help reconstruct China after the war with Japan. Such dreams were often unrealized but the pursuit of the goal was impetus enough to expose them to the professional work world.

The location of the film industry in Hollywood provided one of the most unusual sources of income to Chinese American women in Los Angeles. Already, the exotic image of the Chinese had made Chinatown and its residents a commodity to the American society at large. The development of China City near Olvera Street as a tourist attraction in 1940 depended on that image for its income. One woman remembers that as a little girl, she used to sell flowers to tourists, and for an extra penny sing, "God Bless America."

By far, the most lucrative salaries were to be made in the movie industry. Movies with Chinese themes were in great demand at that time. Several Chinese American women, not relied upon by families to produce consistent income, were able to establish themselves in high-risk careers, the like of which they would not have imagined themselves in before. *The Red Lantern* (1919), the *Good Earth* (1936), and later *Love is a Many Splendored Thing* (1950) initiated the careers of actresses Anna May Wong, actress Beulah Quo and casting director Bessie Loo. For the many Chinese Americans who were extras in these films, the main incentive was the good pay. Being in the movies was not considered by them to be glamorous. Back in China, the entertainment field was in fact seen as having low status. Eventually, however, the promise of extra income and the prominence that the industry had in American society led many Chinese to overlook those old ideas and turn to film as a career.

Wages

It is difficult to assess what the wages of Chinese American women were in comparison to Chinese American men or to the population at large. According to the Chinese American men who were in the work force in the 1920's, salaries were low at about $10-$15 per week or $520-$780 a year. By comparison, the Bureau of Commerce placed the national average salary for a full time worker in 1923 at $1,548. In the late 1930's, more Chinese American women were working at salaried jobs. One who was working in the office or in the garment factory might earn $18-$25 a week or $900-$1,200 a year. The 1940 census placed the median wage earned by the average full-time female worker in the urban Western states at $800-$999 a year. It would appear that the Chinese woman was earning close to the median income of the average female worker if she were working twelve months out of the year. It is quite possible, however, that due to the tendency for Chinese American women to job-hop that this was not the case.

The family income could be supplemented, however, by home labor, and the more family members that participated, the higher the income. Restaurants might deliver walnuts to willing Chinese homes, either to be cracked at 25 cents an hour, or to be sorted into seven grades at 6 cents per pound. Though the practice was not widespread, some families even made wine at home, selling it for $6 a gallon. With this extra income, Chinese American women could manage the family's living expenses with more confidence, though they felt that it was easier at that time anyway since it seemed that everything was cheaper. They fondly remember that hamburgers only cost 5 cents and rent was $20 a month.

In the early 1940's, better jobs became available to the Chinese. A Chinese woman working as a federal civil servant earned about $36 a week and a reporter $45 a week. A good salary was about $200 a month, with expenses being about $30-$35 for an average 2 to 3 bedroom house.

Experiences at Work

The following sections focus on the working experiences of the Chinese American women in the Oral History Project as told by them. Their contributions to the economy will be discussed in the areas of the professions, the entertainment industry, education, family businesses, the clerical and sales area, and light and heavy industry.

Professional Chinese American Women

The first Chinese American women professionals in Los Angeles were pioneers in their own right. Even though there was little encouragement and few role models, and despite both covert and overt forms of discrimination, they became successful career women. Most of the careers chosen were in the helping professions or in the business arena: social worker, nurse, teacher, real estate agent or insurance agent. But there were also a colorful variety of unusual and unique professions that come nowhere close to any stereotype of a Chinese American woman. Included in these are an aviatrix, a beer distributor, a journalist, a circus performer, and a casting agent.

Typically, these women do not see themselves as extraordinary, yet all were able to develop great self-motivation and independence in an environment that generally discouraged it. These women were able to balance the demands of a family that relied

Grace Chow, the only Asian American woman to win the Will G. Farrell Award for her outstanding performance as an insurance agent and for her distinguished and unselfish services to others.

— Courtesy of Grace Chow

heavily on the mother as the focal point and guide with the mobile requirements of their jobs. Many of these women did not know that they were going to have the careers that they did. Some, for instance, were educated to be social workers, but couldn't find jobs, and ended up as teachers and actresses. Others, when forced to support themselves, used the background they had in business or other occupations. Many of the women were in other jobs prior to their profession — selling, typing, and packing.

These professional jobs demanded that the Chinese American woman act aggressively and be able to deal with non-Chinese business and social contacts. Such is the case with Grace Chow, who was an insurance agent. When her husband became ill, Chow decided to accept an offer to sell for Occidental Life. She was so successful that within seven years, she had qualified for life membership in the insurance field's Million Dollar Round Table. The honor resulted from her sales of a million dollars worth of insurance three years in succession. At the time, there were few Chinese working in insurance. In her company, there were only ten to fifteen, and only two or three of them were women. While it would seem difficult to step into such a career, Chow's background prepared her for it. She had been perfecting her sales techniques while selling for her husband's tea company.

Selling insurance led Chow to travel cross country and deal extensively with non-Chinese. She says her success lay in her philosophy of hard work. "If I sold more, I knew I had worked harder. Many companies were surprised to know that a Chinese woman could bring in so much business. (Because of my sales), I was accepted by the non-Chinese. It was the Chinese who did not accept me at first because a woman was supposed to stay at home and take care of the family and husband, and not go out into the business world."

Lilly Lee made her first million as a real estate investor after age forty. Her background stands in stark contrast to her present career. Like other Chinese American women growing up in Los Angeles Chinatown in the 1930's, she was taught to be an obedient daughter and never talk loudly. Her family did provide her with a good education, but only so that she could be a legal secretary, an occupation they thought appropriate for Chinese daughters.

But Lee's husband, wanting to be able to retire at age 40, encouraged her to get her real estate license. She had not intended to use it part-time and it was not until she got divorced that she utilized her license to its fullest capacity. Not concerned about whether she liked the business or not, she plowed straight into it.

Lee started by selling small apartments, worked her way up to vice-president of a non-Chinese firm, and eventually opened up her own office in Beverly Hills. Lee feels that her background gave her the philosophy that allowed her to succeed, but that she also had to develop her own individual philosophy. "The Chinese in me helped me to be successful because it taught me to be patient. Being humble and respectful also gives the Chinese a better view of a situation." But of her individual philosophy, she says, "I went from one business to another because many of them did not work out. I did not dwell on the fact that they did not work out. I always thought very positively. I never thought there was anything that could not be done. Once I had a goal in my mind, I thought of ways to accomplish it instead of ways it could not be accomplished."

One of the most unique and unusual professions entered by a Chinese American woman was that of the aviatrix. Katherine Cheung was at the height of popularity in 1932 because of her daring performances as one of the outstanding woman pilots of her time. Born in Canton, she arrived in America originally to study music at the University of Southern California, but became fascinated with flying when she received a letter from her girlfriend in China. It said that there was a flying school opening up in Canton, but that it wasn't open to females. Cheung reflected on the fact that she was in California, where many opportunities were open to women. At that moment, she decided to pursue flying. In 1932, she was quoted as saying, "I don't see any valid reason why a Chinese woman can't be as good a pilot as anyone else. We drive automobiles — why not fly airplanes?"

At first her family was reluctant, but they became avid supporters after she took them on a flight. By age 22, with 12½ hours of flying instruction, she was off for her first solo. She obtained her private license as a pilot, and developed her skills in navigational flying, acrobatics and cross-country races. In national contests for women pilots, she was often one of the top winners. Her skill as a pilot was recognized when she was admitted into the 99 club, an exclusive, nationwide organization of women flyers

Katherine Cheung, outstanding Chinese American woman pilot, with the 99 Club.
Ms. Cheung is second from the left, rear row.
— Courtesy of Katherine Cheung

with Amelia Earhart as president. Needless to say, she was the first Chinese member of this club.

As Cheung's accomplishments were often noted in both the Chinese and non-Chinese press, she was a well-known figure in the Chinese community and the object of much pride. This admiration culminated in monetary contributions by members of Chinatowns across the country toward her dream of finally owning her own plane.

Another woman with a colorful life was Louise Leung Larson, who was a newspaper journalist. Raised in a family in which parents encouraged her efforts and contact with Americans, and having always liked words and creative writing, she graduated from USC in 1926 in journalism and English. Her first break came when an article she wrote was accepted by the *Los Angeles Record,* the smallest newspaper at that time in Los Angeles. The article was on the Chinese custom of having a celebration for a baby after the first month of birth. Accompanied by a photo of her nephew, it ended up on the front page. Thereafter, Larson was offered a job as a reporter at $20 a week.

It was unusual for a reporter to be both female and Chinese at that time, but Larson was able to learn quickly by working hard. "Working in journalism made me more aggressive. One has to be pretty thick-skinned. I got used to having doors slammed in my face." Since there were few staff at her newspaper, she covered all the County government offices in the Hall of Justice, thus having the opportunity to report the big stories. She stayed there for three years, then worked at the *San Francisco News,* and then at the *Chicago Times,* where she met and married her husband, another reporter. Finally, she returned to Los Angeles to settle down to family life, occasionally doing some freelance work for the *Los Angeles Times.*

In 1942, however, Larson was asked by the *Los Angeles Daily News* to cover Madame Chiang Kai-shek, who was coming to Los Angeles. Larson did so successfully and was then offered a job as a regular reporter, covering general assignments. She stayed there for three years until her daughter was born. She was the only Chinese working on that paper, and was paid about $45 a week. The only other Chinese working in journalism in Southern California was a man working at the *Los Angeles Herald.*

Family illnesses and divorce later demanded that she find a job. Larson went back on the job as a reporter for the Santa Monica *Evening Outlook* in 1957. Covering Malibu and Topanga, she stayed on the job for thirteen years until her retirement.

Larson eventually grew accustomed to working in a non-Chinese environment like journalism. In fact, to some degree, she felt that being Chinese in a non-Chinese environment worked to her advantage. In Chicago, she felt she was treated better because her co-workers had not known many Chinese and were pleased that she could speak and write an English sentence! She exceeded their expectations and was eventually given the best assignments.

A significant number of Chinese American women aspired to professions in public service as a nurse, social worker or teacher. Steady income was part of the incentive. A nurse in the 1940's could make $180 a month before the state board examinations and even more after passing them. For social workers, an incentive was to return to China and help in its reconstruction after the war with Japan. Meanwhile, however, in Los Angeles, it was difficult to get hired as a social worker. When Marjorie Dong graduated from Chapman College with her degree in the 1930's, she received no job offers in Los Angeles or China. She went to San Francisco and worked with Chinese orphans and was only compensated with room and board. Jobs just were not available for Chinese social workers, so she made her way back to Los Angeles, and became an elementary school teacher.

Beulah Quo, encouraged by parents who stressed the value of education, went to the University of California at Berkeley for a degree in social work, and graduated from the University of Chicago with a Masters degree in sociology in 1947. There, she completed one of the earliest studies on the occupations and careers of Chinese Americans from 1920 to 1940. She and her husband were both interested in going back to China to help with reconstruction. They did go back, but returned because of the revolution in China in 1949. Quo worked for a year in social welfare when her career turned in an unexpected direction toward the movie industry.

Entertainment Industry

The exotic image that the Chinese held for the American public enabled some to earn minor to major portions of their income this way. The popularity of the Chinese culture created jobs such as teaching Caucasians to play mah jong or to use the wok. One woman recalls posing in Chinese clothes for artists painting portraits at the university. "These dresses we wore were from China. We got them from various people who would bring them back from a trip to China, but ate so much on the boat that they could no longer fit the clothes."

In the early 1930's, one young woman joined the L.G. Barnes Circus, which had its winter quarters in Culver City. They were looking for a Chinese girl to play the Little Prince in "Aladdin and his Wonderful Lamp." Financial benefits were the greatest enticement: "I was making $75 a week while the girls working in department stores were only earning $18 a week." There were other Chinese employed as helpers and one Chinese male who was the "Chinese Giant," standing over seven feet tall. She described her job: "I took all these little midgets out of this golden

Movies with Asian themes provided job opportunities for Chinese Americans like child actress Lilly Mu Lee, seen here in the 1930's with Clark Gable.
— Courtesy of Lilly Mu Lee

lantern, and there was this big tree on stage, and a big part of it would fall down. A fairy queen would come out of the tree."

Hollywood offered the Chinese an easy way to make some money as extras. Films on China or Chinatown were quite popular during the 1920's and 30's, although such popularity did not indicate that any of the portrayals would be accurate or any more than one-dimensional. Chinese American women seemed to fare well in this business, perhaps because they were able to endure the erratic income. Since there was less pressure on them to have a career, they had the flexibility to almost stumble into an occupation which the Chinese traditionally held in low regard.

Young and old alike were extras in "casts of thousands." One woman remembers being in her first movie at the age of three, in *The Good Earth* in 1936. While being in the movies was not acceptable, the family needed the money, so she continued to be in the movies until she was a teenager. "It was fun for me to go to the studios because I did not have to go to school. There was a school at the studios. I didn't have to know any special skills, but just follow the directions given by the director." Her family stopped her from continuing at age twelve because they felt she should start focusing on her education.

When it became apparent that movies with Chinese themes were going to be steady business in the late 1930's, some Chinese were asked to be casting agents. Amongst those asked were Bessie Loo and Lillie Louie, and their job was to find the appropriate Chinese Americans for the roles or background scenes that the studios required.

At first, employment was informal and no records were kept. At that time, one would be paid $3-$4 a day. But when the Screen Guild came into being in 1930, members got between $10-$20 a day. Wages were computed with overtime, and was adjusted higher if one wore one's own wardrobe. Later, a Screen Actors Guild was formed for those who spoke one line or more. Few depended solely on working in the movies for their income. Still, the money was relatively good; working one week in the movies could exceed the income from working three months at another type of job.

Film work was quite erratic and unstable. Lilly Louie says, "We worked on call. There was no warning and each job was different. We could not plan ahead. (On) one of the coldest nights, we worked on a film in Chinatown. In other words, we would not have the right clothing for the weather. As for speaking parts, we had laughing only and speaking in groups."

For casting directors, the work was also unpredictable. Louie continues, "There were days we did not dare leave the phone for fear of losing a call." Such work would have to be supplemented with other income because "sometimes months and years would go by between calls for film work." The casting director acted not only as go-betweens, but also as advocates for the Chinese. Louie says, "It took some negotiation to convince the movie people that we were always here and when there is a street crowd, there should be a sprinkling of us in there. With that, more work was allocated to the Chinese."

Bessie Loo began her lifelong career as a talent agent and actress when she first appeared in the "Good Earth" in 1936.

— Courtesy of Bessie Loo

The movie industry was not the first occupation of choice for those involved. For two of the most prominent women in the industry, Beulah Quo and Bessie Loo, there were other goals in their lives. Quo was in social work. For Bessie Loo, a prominent talent agent, her original goal was to be a teacher. She majored in education at UCLA, and was in fact teaching, but had to give up her job when she got married. At that time, schools did not allow married women to teach.

She did show an early interest in the stage, which was something her parents did not appreciate. This led to her being one of four Chinese to get a contract for appearing in the *Good Earth* in 1936. She was asked by Central Casting to be a casting director, which she agreed to under the conditions that she could work at home and take care of her children at the same time. She also acted as an assistant director, helping to direct the Chinese extras, who sometimes numbered in the hundreds.

Being an agent was exciting, demanding and sometimes financially lucrative. Loo was paid by the film company, and also took a 10% commission from the extras. Demands were sudden and sometimes enormous, requiring her at times to get as many as 500 extras. For help, Loo often called on the Chinese Cinema Club, which was located on Main and Alameda and was a center for Chinese actors and members of the Screen Extras Guild. Oftentimes, these same people could be seeking her out. Some Chinese, after losing money from playing at the lottery all night, would call her for a job at 5 A.M.

Loo saw advocacy as part of her job. Because of stereotyping, the Chinese were rarely given very important parts, but Loo would try to convince the movie moguls, "If you give them (the Chinese) the part, they will show you, we can and do emote." Loo also tried to get some players to boycott films that portrayed the Chinese in derogatory ways, such as the *Opium Eater* and *Shanghai Gesture*.

It was through Bessie Loo that Beulah Quo inadvertently got her start in acting. Loo asked Quo to be the Chinese language tutor for Jennifer Jones in *Love is a Many Splendored Thing* in

1950. The director of that film, Henry King, asked Quo to play the part of Jones' aunt. After that feature role, she got offers to do many more character roles.

The fact that Quo got into acting late in her life saved her from the opposition of her parents. "If I had started out being an actress, maybe it would have been a different thing to my parents. But they did not object to my acting career, and in fact, enjoyed watching me in my films." Nor did it get in the way of family life, since she did not work as frequently and thus was able to work her schedule out with her husband, "a traditional person who likes his meals on time." Being accepted as a professional actress, however, did take some getting used to by friends.

The challenge of acting and the opportunity that the media provides is what kept Quo in the field. She refined her art, and continued to act in such commercially successful films as the *Sand Pebbles*, but also started producing public affair shows and documentaries. From 1969 to 1975, she produced Asian American television shows first for KCOP and then KNBC. During that period, in 1974, she produced a documentary on James Wong Howe for which she won an Emmy, becoming the first Asian woman to win such an award. Getting to this level in prominence was not easy. "Building status as an (Asian) actress is difficult. There are so few roles that you don't get a chance to build a career. Besides that, it requires aggressiveness to get what one wants and to know what to do."

An ongoing question for Chinese Americans in the 1930's was the nature of the portrayals of the Chinese. There are a wide range of opinions as to how derogatory the images were. Some feel that the characterizations were accurate in that the Chinese were indeed servants and working in laundries; others wrote off such portrayals as "fantasy". But many felt that the portrayals were uniformly one-dimensional, with the Chinese boxed into roles as villains, waiters or menial laborers. Perhaps the Chinese felt that they could not protest or that few would listen to them. However, says Bessie Loo, "after the Screen Extras Guild was formed, the Chinese were more vocal (about these portrayals)."

Such mixed feelings are reflected in attitudes toward the preeminent Chinese American actress of the 20's and 30's, Anna May

Wong. A well-known figure of the silent film era, she played maids, orphans and Chinese daughters of villains. She had the notoriety of being perhaps the most well-known Asian of her time. There is some disagreement on the value of her fame. Some felt that she played mostly straight roles and only a few derogatory ones. Others admired her for her beauty alone. And still others felt strongly about the stereotypical image she presented. As one woman said, "The parts she portrayed were not good for Chinese. She made reality more sinister." Nevertheless, Anna May Wong demonstrated that a Chinese American woman could attain stature in American society, though that stature was clearly not made on her own terms.

Education

The field of education reluctantly opened its doors to Chinese American women after World War II. It is not surprising that teaching was popular for Chinese American women considering the traditional respect that Chinese hold for education. However, discriminatory practices made it difficult for many of the first aspiring teachers to fulfill their goals.

Caroline Chan was the first Chinese American school teacher in Los Angeles. A true pioneer in all respects, she was also one of the first Chinese American women to attend the University of Southern California, where she got her bachelors degree in English, and the first Chinese woman in Delta Kappa Gamma, a national society for remedial education. It was in the 1920's that she started working as a teacher at Los Angeles' Ninth Street School, an elementary school that needed a Chinese-speaking staff person who could communicate with Chinese parents from downtown's produce market district. Chan had to deal with racial prejudice continuously both from her teachers in her days as a student and from her fellow teachers as she began working. American society was simply not used to seeing Chinese American women in leadership roles.

Life was lonely as a Chinese American female student. While she got her degree in home economics in 1936 at a university in Reno, Nevada, Bernice Sam knew only two other Chinese men and no Chinese women on campus. The resentment that she felt

from her white schoolmates caused her to feel uneasy. Marjorie
Dong received her degree in sociology at Chapman College in
1932, but in her four years in college knew only two other Chinese students.

Chinese American women often were responsible for financing
themselves through school since sons were usually given the
priority for education by the family. This left many Chinese
American women little alternative but to take menial jobs. Dong,
for instance, cleaned and cooked for a UCLA instructor two or
three times a week.

A shortage of teachers was the main impetus for Dong being
hired as one of the first Asian teachers in the Norwalk School
District, where she taught second grade until her retirement. She
enjoyed her career and got along well with fellow teachers and
students. However, she felt that the administrators were prej-
udiced against her because of her race.

The accomplishments of the earliest Chinese American women
in education are astounding considering the barriers during that
time period. Wen Hui Chung Chen was one of the first professors of Chinese descent at any Los Angeles university, the University of Southern California. She had received her college education in Beijing in 1931, eventually obtaining her doctorate in
sociology from the University of Southern California in 1952.
Chen dedicated her education to the improvement of conditions
for Chinese in both China and America. During her graduate
years, she returned to China several times, trying to improve the
social conditions in that country. In 1946-7, she was professor of
the Christian College of Fujien, serving as an administrator in a
time of much chaos after the war. Upon her return to the United
States, she commenced teaching part time in the sociology department at USC while finishing her dissertation. Her home often
served as refuge for the few Chinese students on campus at that
time. Because of Chen's position at the university, she often
served as a leader and representative of the Chinese American
community, and as a link to the black and civil rights movement,
to which she feels the Chinese American community owes much

Dr. Wen Hui Chung Chen at her master's degree graduation in 1940, with her husband and children.

— Courtesy of Wen Hui Chung Chen

for improving the social status of minorities in American society.

The first Chinese American women educators played important roles as models and leaders in their own right. From being among the first Chinese American women to attend American colleges, they went on to break the racial barriers in the field of education and to influence their students who could see first-hand the abilities and potential of Chinese American women.

Family Business

There was many a Chinese woman who played a major role in running the family business. Because societal discrimination limited the opportunities that the Chinese had to get salaried jobs outside the community, many turned to small business as a means of income, operating restaurants, produce markets, laundries, and art-curio shops. These small business ventures could survive, however, only on the unpaid labor of its family members. Thus, Chinese women's labor power was quite integral to the success of the business, emphasizing her importance and allowing her to work side by side with her husband.

Working in the family business began early; many of these women would start work as children and continue up until marriage. They were usually not paid a salary, but given a regular allowance. Bernice Leung's experience was typical; her father owned a restaurant in which all the children worked during the Depression years. Leung recalls that she wasn't the best waitress, but, she says, "I tried!" Despite the fact that her father relied on the labor power of his children and wife, he warned his daughter not to get into the business because, "When you get in, you are stuck with no holidays and no chance of having fun."

Leung later continued in the restaurant business despite the warnings. She married a man who worked in a family-owned restaurant in which she was expected to contribute. Working alongside various members of her husband's family, she served as waitress and dishwasher. From the restaurant's opening in 1947 to its closing some 25 years later, Leung felt it was her duty to help in the business whenever she could even if she were holding other jobs.

Most of the women remember clearly the long hours in running any small business. Florence Hoy and her husband opened a grocery store in Venice in the Depression years, and didn't close their doors until 1961. They lived in the house behind the store, working in the store 6½ days a week from 7 A.M. to 7 P.M. The demanding schedule didn't allow her to take vacations or attend socials or picnics.

Yet working in all these small businesses without pay was not seen by these women as drudgery as much as their duty in order to help their family survive economically. And in some cases the training that they got by working those many years in the business helped them to take up more challenging roles. When Stella Louis' husband left for a long trip to China, she had to manage their small grocery store by herself. Because it was getting to be difficult to compete with supermarkets, she made the decision to convert the store to an art shop with Chinese herbs, clothes, and other merchandise that could attract the booming tourist business. Louis' experience reflects the small but growing number of Chinese women who had developed the confidence and skill to open up their own shops as did Dorothy Siu, who opened up a silk flower shop, the "Flower Hut" in China City in 1938.

Through these small businesses, Chinese American women learned skills as varied as waitressing, cashiering, accounting, and business management. Their lives included punishing hours, little rest and for some, many greasy dishes. This is but a sample of sacrifices and contributions that Chinese women made to their family enterprises, paving the way for them to be considered full partners in the building of their ethnic community.

Sales

A large proportion of Chinese American women found positions in the expanding industries of clerking and sales in the 1940's and 50's. These women were the secretaries, sales clerks, file clerks, operators, and bookkeepers who composed the backbones of government agencies and the business world. These pioneering women introduced a minority presence into the white-collar world.

Few Chinese women worked as clerks in the 1910's, but those that did were working in such jobs as stockroom inventory. Such jobs did not pay much. For instance, Stella Louis worked at the National Dollar Store, where she received $3 a week, which did not amount to much since her commuting expenses were $3.50 a month.

It was in the 1930's and 40's that a clear trend started to emerge. Young Chinese American women, in their teens or early twenties, started working at department stores to earn an income, but were offered very little opportunities except in very modest positions with low public visibility. They were usually put in the backrooms as stackers or as stock girls who would keep merchandise in order. Dorothy Siu remembers that even though the company that she worked for sold Chinese souvenirs, they didn't trust the Chinese to work until the 1940's; she was restricted to working in the repairs department restringing beads.

The only time when Chinese women would be in the public eye in a department store is when they were used to promote an exotic image. Because the United States had high commercial and political interests in China, the American public had become fascinated with the "Orient". Thus, Lillie Louis was hired at Blackstone, the forerunner to the May Company, to teach mah jong to Caucasian customers. Required to wear a bright red Chinese dress, she was supposed to encourage them to buy a set as she explained the game. The customers didn't know that Louis had to quickly learn the game herself before taking the job.

The shortage of workers during World War II opened up many clerical positions for Chinese American women. Some worked directly for the U.S. Army. Others started working in government agencies such as the Department of Agriculture, and the Federal Housing Administration. The salary of $36 a week was adequate for that time period.

The influx of Chinese American women into clerical positions during the war years brought them into contact with the non-Chinese world during a period when discrimination against Asians was high. Some of the women felt the effects of such attitudes through unfair labor practices. When she was looking for a job, Lillian Fong encountered many companies that would not even give her an application form. In 1947, Bernice Leung was the first Chinese to work for Western Auto Supplies as a secretary, but her hiring was so controversial that an executive meeting was held just to discuss it. After six months, she knew she had proven herself to be a good worker when the executives asked her to recommend other Chinese women to fill a new secretarial position. Leung still remembers with satisfaction her reply to them: "Well, not for the kind of salary you offer."

Many of the Chinese American women who worked in clerical positions did so most of their lives, though they often switched from one job to another. For instance, May Lum worked in a candy store, a mink store, and then worked for 20 years at the White House Department Store doing alterations.

While some women broke into the non-Chinese general labor force, other women worked in clerical positions within the Chinese community. Some stayed in Chinatown because they were limited by language in their search for outside jobs. Others worked with Chinese because their bilingual skills were useful, especially for Chinese professionals. One woman worked for a Chinese doctor, taking medicine to patients and explaining their use to them, and another worked for a Chinese American lawyer whose clientele were mainly Chinese. And there were those who were clerks, but also served as translators for the small business owners who did not know English, as in the case of one woman who worked for a Chinese art store and wrote checks for the owner.

Light and Heavy Industry

The need to supplement the family income led Chinese American women to jobs in light and heavy industry. Such jobs oftentimes required great perseverance in order to deal with the adverse conditions on the job. Mass production in both kinds of industry place Chinese women in close working relationship with a wide spectrum of society, forcing the women to learn how to deal with people of different races and backgrounds. Of those who worked in this area, most were concentrated in light rather than heavy industry, and more specifically, in the garment industry. But there were some Chinese American women who did work in heavy industry as defense workers during World War II.

The garment industry was not always prominent as it is in contemporary Los Angeles. Historically centralized in New York, it slowly made its way to areas like Los Angeles because of the great availability of semiskilled labor and the proximity of the factory to the place where the final product was to be marketed. Eventually Los Angeles became part of a growing national market, first starting off in casual wear and eventually expanding to all areas of the national market. Initially, too, workers in the garment industry were not dominated by females as it is now. It was only after the turn of the century that female operators became a prominent element in Chinatown factories.

The first Chinese American women to become garment workers in Los Angeles were in the 1930's. Many of the shops were small and were located in central Los Angeles, attracting a variety of ethnic groups. Chinese American women saw the garment industry as a way of earning an income when many other avenues were closed due to language barriers. For some women in these early years, sewing was a means to supplement income until a primary source of income could be found, such as a family business. Thus in 1938, Oak Yip Gee started working in the garment industry for one or two years before the family opened a restaurant. Other women, however, did not have such choices to make in their lives. May Lum recalls that her mother sewed to support the entire family. Being able to sew both at home and at the factory was popular among Chinese women because of the flexibility it allowed in taking care of the children.

The income from sewing was not high, but it was steady. Lillian Fong earned $18 a week during the 1940's. She was the only Chinese working in an American company called Sandy's Sports Wear. Rose Wong worked in both American and Chinese shops, first working at the Diamond Shirt Company, making buttonholes for 50 cents a shirt, and later working in a Chinese dress shop at Figueroa and Wilshire.

The garment industry was revived as an occupation of choice for the many women who came to the United States from China during the 1950's as a result of the War Brides Act. Faced with language and cultural barriers, many of these women came to rely on the garment industry for their steady job for a time span that lasted decades for some. They approached the job pragmatically, knowing that they had to do something to help their family survive economically.

Sui-Sim Tom Yee started sewing as soon as she arrived in Los Angeles Chinatown in 1955; the job lasted for 23 years. The money from her job went to support her children and their future education. At a wage of 75 cents an hour, there wasn't much money to spread around. Since her starting salary wasn't much, she survived by working longer hours. It became an expectation that, "I always did more." Gradually, toward the end of these 23 years, wages went up to $2.50 an hour.

Yee recalls how slow she was at sewing in the beginning. "When I first started, I had to learn how to sew. I took clothes apart and put it together again. They have patterns for you to look at. There was someone there to teach you." Conditions in the factory required steady and hard work, and treatment in the factories varied. The owner of Yee's factory was a white man whom she considered to have treated her very well. To Yee's amazement, he provided the workers with health benefits — unheard of in China. "If you had any accidents, insurance would give you a bit of money. I was careless on my way to work, fell and injured my hand, and had to go to the hospital. I went to this white hospital; it was the most expensive one. They set the bones, and I didn't have to spend a single penny."

Life may have been hard, but Yee takes pride in her stamina and capacity to work hard. Even though she is now retired, she says "I still think of going back there to work. (They say to me), 'Come back, come back to work!' I say, 'I haven't done it in such a long time, my eyes are no good any longer, my energy and strength aren't up to it.'"

Working in the factory exposed Yee to many different ethnic groups. "All sorts of people . . . Mexicans, Blacks and Chinese. Now there are only a few Chinese. A while back there were about 30 Chinese! They worked in two sections. On one side, they sewed skirts and slacks; on the other side, they sewed blouses and jackets. (Still, my friends) are mostly Chinese."

Less known than the story of women in the garment industry is that of women in heavy industry. It was at the Douglas El Segundo plant that Rose Wong became the Chinese Rosie the Riveter. In the 1940's, her girlfriend took her down to the plant for an application and interview. She thought it would be a "different kind of job," and after going through a security check, was hired. She then stayed on the job for twenty years until her retirement.

When she first worked at Douglas, she had a lab job making spring gauze and was isolated from others. She changed to the job of soldering wires, thus bringing her into contact with others in the plant. No matter what the post, she took pride in what she did. As a solderer, she learned her job fast, and since it was the only work of its kind being done in the company, she tried to do it well. Despite the fact that she was the smallest worker at the plant, she was known for doing excellent work. "When the inspector arrived, everybody asked who did the job that I did. My job always passed — it never failed."

She was then moved to a welding/riveting job. At this time she was paid 60 cents an hour and 65 cents when working the night shift. By the time she retired, she was getting $3.75 an hour. Wages, though not high, were secure; it was the working conditions that took the most effort to overcome. There were very few Asians; in fact, she can remember only two. It was no surprise that she had to face the problems of male chauvinism and racism. Wong was always mistaken for being Japanese, taking comments from other workers that the Japanese should be put back into camp. It was when she became a welder/riveter that she especially encountered a predominantly male work setting. In one of the incidents she remembers most vividly, one of the males tried to provoke her by throwing a buck ball at her. She learned however that she could not take such abuse passively. She threw a buck ball back at him, reported him to the supervisor, and was never bothered again.

Building Community

MARJORIE LEE

The first Chinese women in Los Angeles were not only few in number, but were also isolated from each other and American society. Their husbands or fathers did not allow them to leave their homes for fear of being kidnapped or losing propriety. Family and work obligations did not permit them to break away and socialize among themselves or with "Americans." Chinese women in America sought each other's company and companionship in a society marked by prejudice and in a family dominated by men.

As the number of Chinese women in America gradually increased, a need for camaraderie grew among themselves through both informal and formal relationships. Eventually, an awareness of their civic responsibilities towards both China and America evolved. The wars with Japan and World War II prompted greater involvement in both the Chinese American community and the prevailing community in Los Angeles.

Geographic, economic, and cultural impediments prevented organizing at first. Since the Chinese American community has always been dispersed over the vast metropolis of Los Angeles, development of strong ties between families was difficult. In addition, free time and leisure activities were considered luxuries in a community struggling to survive. Marge Ong remembers that in her youth, she had no free time. After attending American school during the day, she attended Chinese school at her father's insistence. She also was expected to help her mother in housework and care for her seven younger brothers and sisters. Beyond that, there was work to be done at the family restaurant. Ong's greatest task was to find some "free" time just to do her school work. However, she remembers that her brothers were permitted more freedom; as a girl, Marge had little opportunity to cultivate friendships or activities outside the family.

Historic events, such as the women's suffrage movement in the United States, the 1911 Republic Revolution and 1919 May Fourth Movement in China, and World War II, shaped the social consciousness of women. Within this context, Chinese American women, both immigrant and second generation, thrust themselves into active, precedent-setting roles in social and community activities. They were motivated by a strong sense of patriotism to both China and America, as well as growing convictions toward individual freedom and a potential never before permitted in traditional Chinese society. Consequently, they found themselves taking leadership roles in forming their own organizations, such as the Women's New Life Movement Association and the Los Angeles Women's Club, and in organizing activities in community fraternal organizations that had traditionally been for men only.

During the early years between 1900 and 1930, most of the women residing in the Chinese community of Los Angeles had recently emigrated from China. The majority of them were typically encumbered with family and school obligations, and were in no position to spend time and money on organizational activities. It was not until the start of the second generation Chinese, from about the 1930's to 1950's, that women began to engage in organized activities outside the home. Finally, during the postwar years between 1950 and 1965, many Chinese American families moved out of the Chinatown area to live, work, and establish new relationships within the mainstream of Los Angeles life.

The Early Years 1900-1930

The Confucian tradition which gave order and structure to the Chinese family began to lose its influence on American soil, as the first generation struggled to balance the two cultures and as the second generation came of age. This was especially true with respect to the role and function of young Chinese women in the family and society. The past could no longer bind the Americanized Chinese girls to home, family, or traditional Chinese culture. They yearned for a role and lifestyle different from the ones that their mothers experienced in China and America.

Drawn towards interests outside the family, many younger Chinese American women sought each other's friendship. For those girls who had a more financially secure background or liberal parents, clubs and socializing among peers became a reality. At the start of the 1930's, an assortment of activities, interests, and hobbies evolved in the Los Angeles Chinese American community, bringing the girls into further contact with Western thoughts, ideas, and values. Church involvement, volunteer service, and social activities attracted the girls who were already kept busy by American school, the Chinese language school, and domestic family obligations. Clubs, such as the Chinese Girls Glee Club, the Mei Wah and Kuan Ying, were formed to stimulate friendships and social service among the girls who had the spare time. Sports, especially basketball and tennis be-

Los Angeles Chinese Girls Glee Club in 1931.
— Courtesy of Peter SooHoo, Jr.

came a very popular pastime in Los Angeles. Some girls formed clubs of their own, such as the Lowa Auxiliary and Cathayettes, to play basketball.

At the start, there was hesitation and fear, shared by both men and women, who felt that such outside commitments would weaken home life and disrupt harmonious family relationships. However, the key objective of such groups was to broaden the experiences of Chinese American women, without interfering with existing responsibilities in their homes. It was only in cooperation with their fathers, husbands, and brothers, that they could expand their social roles. Mrs. Lily Chan was convinced that had her husband not been so supportive and understanding of her many activities outside the home, she would not have had the time or freedom: "You see, I had two babies and a home to take care of. How fortunate I was to have such a wonderful husband. Not many women were as lucky as I."

The War Years 1930-1950

The call for aid and support of China during the Sino-Japanese War and World War II explains the evolution of many girls' and women's organizations from 1930 to 1945.

Japanese aggression against China began in 1931 and culminated in the outbreak of the Sino-Japanese war in 1937. With reports of the sufferings and starvation of war victims and orphaned children, and of resistance movements in China, Chinese American women joined fraternal organizations in America to help China defend herself. They became active participants, and also highly visible leaders at the forefront of these war relief efforts.

One such group was the Women's New Life Movement Association, founded to raise money to help the orphans in China. It started in the summer of 1938, when Madame Chiang Kai-shek held a conference of 48 women leaders in China to discuss strategies in mobilizing the women of China and America to help win the war against Japanese aggression. As a result of this meeting, 33 affiliations of the New Life Movement were inaugurated in China, and 10 branches were formed in America.

The Association's activities included fund-raising for war-time relief and providing educational and cultural activities for the women. The first president of the Los Angeles New Life Chapter,

Los Angeles chapter of the national organization, the Chinese Women's New Life Movement Association. Early 1950's.

— Courtesy of Henry S. Quan

Lily Chan, estimated they raised nearly $2,000-$3,000 each year for war relief. Because of the nature of the cause, New Life reached a cross-section of women in and out of Chinatown, both English and non-English speaking, American-born and China-born. Further, it became an important catalyst to the formation of future Chinese American women's and girl's clubs and associations. Many of the women's first apprehensions to joining this organization were due to fear that it would endanger their obligations to their families and create family strife. However, the women leaders of the New Life Movement in both China and America soon recognized that their place should not only be in

the home, but also in the community. Chan felt that, "We mobi-
lized women to do civic affairs, breaking the ice in our community. We weren't ERA or anything, but we encouraged women to
get involved. I think we helped give women the push, because
many of them have since formed or helped to form other women's
groups. We saw the need and knew our efforts could help."

The New Life Movement wasn't the only group engaged in
such activities. Along with the Women's Auxiliary to the Chinese
American Citizens Alliance, many Chinese American women and
girls assisted in organizing rallies and boycotts of goods made in
Japan, appealed to women to wear cotton hosiery instead of
Japanese silk stockings, and helped to raise funds to send back
medical supplies and food to China.

It was during this period that a series of fund-raising activities
were planned under the theme, "Bowl of Rice." Second-generation
Chinese American women organized bazaars, fashion shows, and
theatrical and dance productions, in order to raise money, as well
as provide the Chinese American community with entertainment.
In the process, they also acquired leadership, performance, and
organizational skills.

The Mei Wah Club was one such organization. At the outbreak
of the Japanese invasion in China, the Club called all Chinese
youth clubs in Los Angeles to the Nationalist Hall to stage a benefit for war refugees. The Mei Wah girls were in charge of the
program in which a Floradora Sextette, directed by Elsie Yip,
performed a musical dance number. This was only the beginning
of many fund-raising activities which the Mei Wah girls helped
to organize on behalf of the needs of war-torn China.

One event in particular brought them into a new area of involvement to the Chinese community; this was the 1938 Moon
Festival. Considered the first large public assembly and festive
celebration in the Chinese community in Los Angeles, the Festival
was sponsored by the Chinese Consolidated Benevolent Association as a fund-raising effort for the United China Relief. The
three-day celebration and parade was organized as a large war
relief benefit and rally, which included the selection of a Moon
Festival Queen to reign over the Festival's celebration. As a
novelty, David SooHoo, the brother of Peter SooHoo, who was

the founder of Los Angeles' Chinatown, suggested that the Mei Wah girls form a drum corps and perform as the parade's own Chinese musical unit. In just two weeks, twelve Mei Wah girls choreographed, learned their routines, and designed costumes

Originally formed to perform at war relief functions, the Mei Wah Girls Drum Corps became very popular in Los Angeles, winning awards for their skills.
— Courtesy of Peter SooHoo, Jr.

for the parade. Their drum majorette, Barbara Jean Lee, led them in the evening's parade, and the audience was both amazed and excited to see the first performance of a Los Angeles Chinese American girls' drum corps.

Under the direction of David SooHoo, the Corps' performance was so well received that the Los Angeles Chinese Mei Wah Drum Corps was asked to perform at many events, such as the Santa Claus Parade and the opening of the Union Station. The group went on to win awards for its performances at band and drill team competitions.

In 1938, 17 Chinese American youth groups coalesced into one united force called the Los Angeles Federation of Chinese Clubs. Similar to one established in San Francisco the previous year, the

Federation formed in response to the crisis in China and the
need to raise war relief funds for the refugees and the battle-
torn areas. Their purpose reflected their understanding of the
importance of community: "Our elderly long before have coordinated themselves into a centralized society . . . to undertake with
greater effectiveness the crucial tasks of relief, medical aid, etc.
Unity is the watch word."

When the United States entered World War II in 1941 as
China's ally, Chinese American women participated in the war
effort by selling war bonds, caring for and entertaining soldiers,

*Famous actress Anna May Wong was one of the many Chinese American women
working for war relief in 1944.*
                                        — Courtesy of Lilly Mu Lee

and serving in the armed forces. Evidence of the China-U.S.
alliance was seen in the enthusiastic reception given to Madame
Chiang Kai-shek who made a trip across the United States in
1943. Madame Chiang traveled to Los Angeles on March 31, and
was given a warm welcome by the city of Los Angeles. The high-
light of her stay was the last day of her visit, when she made a
public speech at the Hollywood Bowl. Speaking before a packed
arena, she inspired many Chinese American women, both English
and non-English speaking, to join the New Life Movement and

to recognize their civic responsibilities to both China and America. As a result, New Life's membership exceeded 200 that year.

Young women from other clubs, such as the Kuan Ying Club as well as the Mei Wah Club, joined as volunteers to work at the canteen in the building of the old Soo Chow Restaurant on Jung Jing Road. These women appeared at programs and learned first aid. The L.A. Chinese Women's Club assisted at the downtown canteen, near 5th and Olive.

The canteen in New Chinatown was a particularly special focus for the Chinese community. Not only did it entertain the Chinese American servicemen, but also Chinese Nationalist air cadets and soldiers who were in Los Angeles to receive training. About 60 young women, between ages 16 and 18, signed up as junior hostesses, serving coffee, sandwiches, and light refreshments from 4:00 P.M. to 10:00 P.M. on weekdays, and 4:00 P.M. to midnight on Saturdays. After the war, the girls' and women's clubs found other reasons to keep their networks going, and their philanthropic activities were balanced more with social and athletic functions. Those organizations which have survived the quiet post-war years met for service and friendship. They have remembered their past with reunions, anniversary banquets, and engaged in new areas of philanthropic work in both the Chinese American and greater communities in Los Angeles.

The Mainstreaming Years: 1945-1965

The period after World War II saw Chinese American families building lives and molding careers outside the Chinese community. Central to many of the Chinese American women's objectives for involvement outside the Chinese community was the dedication and commitment to improving and enhancing public opinion toward China and overseas Chinese. Many of the women who were versed in English as well as Chinese dialects accepted and arranged speaking engagements to talk about China, Chinese culture, and Chinese Americans. It was important to interpret China and educate those who knew very little about Chinese and Chinese Americans. This was their way of combating the discrimination and racism which plagued the Chinese, especially from the war years to the 1960's.

Many Chinese American women all over the city joined social, volunteer, and philanthropic organizations in which they were the only Chinese American members. Women, such as Lily Chan, Grace Chow, Ella Chung, Beulah Quo, Bessie Loo, and Lily Ho Quon, assumed leadership roles in Girl Scouts, Cub Scouts and Boy Scouts, YWCA's, United Way, USC and Loyola Faculty Wives, churches outside of Chinatown, as well as in various business and professional women's groups.

Most of the Chinese American women who were able to participate and gain memberships in the Caucasian organizations were from very prominent families whose fathers or husbands had become financially successful in America. Consequently, societal, artistic and cultural community involvement in Los Angeles were open only to a few.

In order to better bridge the gap between the larger American community and the Chinese community, Chinese American women channelled their energies into the Los Angeles Women's Club, which became an active member of the California Federation of Women's Clubs in 1947. This was the first time that the Federation invited a non-Caucasian women's organization into its association. Acceptance into this Federation was a major step for this organization, in light of the many years of discrimination and restricted participation in all aspects of American society. Club members felt that American people did not believe that Chinese women were educated and even were graduated from college. Under the Federation's guidance, the L.A. Chinese Women's Club learned how to extend its civic responsibility beyond its own community and improve interracial understanding.

Martha Chow, the club's president in its second year, remembered that the organization started with about 15 ladies — some American-born, some China-born — who wanted to talk about China and promote a better understanding between Chinese and Americans. Chinese American women became members for various reasons. Caroline Chan, one of its charter members, joined for social reasons. Elaine Chan, who joined in 1947, did so because it was an organization that helped people. Members were said to include the wives of local doctors, dentists, attorneys, professors, owners of family-operated businesses, curio shops, restaurants and meat markets. Again, because of the social status of most of its first members, some women felt that the club mainly represented the more wealthy families of the Chinese American community.

With the intent of fostering closer friendships and cooperation among the Chinese American women in Los Angeles, as well as bringing Chinese culture to the American community, the members of this organization raised money for the War Chest and the World YWCA Reconstruction program. They held a Spring Festival and bazaar featuring entertainment, flower arrangements, thus providing opportunities for other Chinese American clubs and organizations to participate and interact. One special activity was their Chinese New Year's Tea, in which the presidents and representatives of all the women's clubs, Chinese and non-Chinese alike, in the Los Angeles Federation were invited to attend. The site of this tea was at a member's home which was ornately decorated in an exquisite Chinese style. The Chinese members would dress themselves in elegant Chinese costumes.

Certain Chinese American women stood out as early advocates for integrating into the Caucasian community. One such woman was the late Lily Ho Quon, whose husband has become one of the most successful businessman in the Chinese American community in Los Angeles. Lily Ho Quon was an outstanding volunteer and philanthropic leader in Los Angeles during the 1940's and 1950's. A graduate of Ginling College in Nanking, the largest and most prestigious women's college in China, as well as the University of Southern California's Music graduate program in 1928, Quon demonstrated interest in many sectors of the arts and culture of Los Angeles. In addition to founding the Los Angeles Chinese Women's Club, she had been president of the International Women's Committee, had held distinguished memberships with the Blue Ribbons of the Music Center, Opera Guild, Beverly

Hills Women's Club, and the Junior Auxiliary of the Jewish Home for the Aged. In 1945, Quon was named the California State's "Mother of the Year" by the Golden Rule Foundation.

Another pioneer contributing to the Los Angeles community was Maye Wong. Wong had worked with the Los Angeles Chamber of Commerce and had belonged to the Ladies' Oriental Shrine of America and the Eastern Star, Hollywood chapter. In the past, she had been president of the Gleason Parliamentary Club, as well as parliamentarian for the Los Angeles Metropolitan District's California Federation of Women's Clubs. Her very active role in this Federation included her efforts, along with Lily Ho Quon's and Martha Chow's, in linking the Chinese Women's Club with the California Federation. For Chinese American women in Los Angeles, this was considered an important step toward integration.

Women's organizations have played a significant role in the lives of many Chinese American women in Los Angeles. Those that have repeatedly appeared in the memories of many Chinese American women in Los Angeles are briefly described in the Appendix.

Conclusion

As Chinese American women gained greater independence, education and social status, they also took major roles in building their community in Los Angeles. The variety of organizations to which they belonged reflected the skillful abilities and strong convictions that these women possessed. Once given the opportunity, Chinese American women were able to contribute to war efforts, to facilitate intercultural relationships, and to help their youth adjust more positively in American society. Through their involvements, they were able to develop their leadership abilities and to develop organizational skills. They did not let the barriers to joining fraternal and Caucasian organizations prevent them from forming their own groups and doing what they could to improve the status of Chinese women in America.

APPENDIX

Major Women's Organizations

Women's New Life Movement Association (1938). Formed out of the New Life Movement initiated by the Kuomintang government, the Women's New Life Movement Association was patriotic in nature. Its purpose was to motivate overseas Chinese women to become educated and to take an interest in international problems, American politics, and the welfare of their local Chinese communities in America. The New Life Movement was part of China's plan for social reform, with one important focus being women's roles. It was anticipated that the Movement would give Chinese women a new opportunity to become participants in important community and national concerns, beyond their traditional roles as housewives and mothers. Women involved in the New Life Movement joined the men's endeavors to support China during the Sino-Japan War. Together, they could, as Lily Chan said, "churn the wheel of progress without jeopardizing the family." In short, this movement gave Chinese American women an opportunity to enter into other social and political arenas of involvement.

The Los Angeles branch was considered the largest, with other sister branches located in San Francisco and Sacramento. After holding several organizing meetings, they held their first official meeting in the fall of 1938, at the Chinese Presbyterian Church on Adams Boulevard. Their motto was, "Propriety, Dedication, Frugality, and Humility." Very active during the war years, its leaders succeeded in mobilizing many Chinese American women in war relief efforts and patriotic activities. Thus, New Life played a crucial role in not only resisting and defeating Japan's aggression against China, but also in building up the identity of women as contributors and dedicated participants in society.

The activities of the organization shifted during peace time to more educational, charitable, and cultural programs, which are still carried out today. Over the years, they have gone to the public schools to talk about China, supported Chinese artists and musicians whenever they came to town, and raised money to award scholarships to promising Chinese American students. Educating people about China and dispelling myths about Chinese and Chinese culture was their way of battling racism and discrimination.

New Life's popularity peaked during the war years and subsequently declined in membership. However, many committed members still meet today at anniversary banquets and reunions, remembering their contributions to Los Angeles and China, as well as the many friendships which were generated throughout the years.

Los Angeles Chinese Women's Club and Juniors (1944). Organized in 1944 and founded by Lily Ho Quon, the Los Angeles Chinese Women's Club was the first organization specifically designed for the needs of Chinese women in America. Modeled after other American women's social clubs, this club attempted to link Chinese American women with the larger society by participating in activities outside the Chinese American community. As Martha Chow claimed, "Our chief aim was for Chinese American women and Caucasian women to get to know each other better."

The objectives of the Club were: 1) to promote fellowship among the Chinese women of Los Angeles; 2) to participate in activities of the Chinese community; and 3) to participate in civic activities for the promotion of international friendship and better understanding. To this end, it joined the California Federation of Women's Clubs in 1947, and was the first non-Caucasian organization to do so. It was an active member of the Federation, engaging in many philanthropic and cultural awareness activities.

In 1949, the organization had the dream of building a central meeting place for its members and other Chinese women's groups. Numerous fund-raising activities were planned that year in order to establish a building fund. Realizing that Los Angeles was a large area in which many women were scattered, the Club felt the urgent need to meet and work out of a central location. Unfortunately, this goal never materialized, because the cost was more than the organization was able to raise.

The Los Angeles Chinese Women's Club is the only women's organization to have survived the war years. Together with their Junior association, it continues to welcome new members who can offer new ideas and energy. It still gives scholarships to young Chinese American men and women interested in furthering their education. Their scholarship fund is raised by selling their popular cookbook, holding luncheons, and putting on many other activities.

In 1953, a Junior component to the Los Angeles Chinese Women's Club was formed as an affiliate of the California Federation by the Senior group for their daughters, who were under the age of 35 years. As two distinct, yet connected organizations, their objectives were similar since they were all members of the Federation. They planned many community service activities and events as did their Senior group.

*Women's Auxiliary, Chinese American Citizens Alliance —
Los Angeles Lodge.* As a fraternal organization, the Chinese American Citizens Alliance (C.A.C.A.) until recently only allowed membership to the men in the community. The idea of the Women's Auxiliary was met with interest by many of the members' wives who automatically took responsibility in planning C.A.C.A.'s activities and efforts anyway. The formation of the Women's Auxiliary gave formal recognition to their efforts and provided them with a structure to organize more efficiently.

Their purpose was "for the promotion of the objectives and purposes of the Chinese American Citizens Alliance, Los Angeles Lodge" A wife of a Lodge member, whether he was living or deceased, was eligible for membership. They assisted the organization in their social programs, prepared refreshments after meetings, and visited the ill in rest homes in Los Angeles.

In 1980, the C.A.C.A.-Los Angeles Lodge, finally opened its membership to women, so the auxiliary was formally dismantled. Ella Chung, the founder of the Women's Auxiliary, and Lily Chan were the first two women to become C.A.C.A. members. Chung was their financial secretary for the last two years, while Chan was the first woman ever to preside as their Lodge's marshal.

Family Fellowship (1952). Beulah Quo, Mary Fung, Elsie Ho, and Nell Hong founded this small, close-knit group which consisted of approximately 24 Chinese American families residing in the greater Los Angeles area. The Fellowship met approximately four times a year to promote a social link to Chinese American families scattered all over the southland area.

The families were from as far west as Brentwood and Malibu, from as far south as Redondo Beach, and as far north as La Crescenta and Sun Valley. Planning activities primarily for the children of these families, the leadership, decision-making, and organization of the Fellowship were assumed entirely by the women.

After 20 years, the Family Fellowship became less active as the children scattered to college, many leaving Los Angeles. However, the ties among the adult members have remained close, and informal attempts have been made since to combine their social reunions with philanthropic activities.

Women's Church (Christian) Auxiliaries. If there was any participation in organizations or clubs outside the home by Chinese women in Los Angeles, it was surely the church that received the greatest involvement. The women's church auxiliaries were organized by women to plan and organize activities for themselves and their social membership.

Some of the first all Chinese churches established in the Los Angeles area were the Chinese Presbyterian and Chinese Methodist Churches in Old Chinatown, Chinese Congregational Church off San Pedro Street, and the Chinese Catholic Center in New Chinatown.

Many of the women formed such auxiliaries to pool their energies together and to become a vital arm of the churches. They planned and organized fund-raisers, luncheons, bazaars, and took care of any other needs of the church. And, when war brides of

Chinese American war veterans arrived in Los Angeles after World War II, many of the auxiliaries took these newly-arrived women on field trips all over Los Angeles to show them where and how to shop, and to familiarize them with what they should know in establishing a family in America.

It is impossible to mention the numerous activities each auxiliary has organized and sponsored in the past. It may be sufficient to simply summarize that these church auxiliaries provided much-needed support to the church and service to the community, and provided informal opportunities for socializing. It was a place where all women, regardless of educational, cultural, or family background, could be a part of some network to talk, sew, and share their lives.

Major Girls' Clubs/Organizations

Mei Wah Club (1931). What had originally been a basketball and athletic club, the Mei Wah Club, meaning "Chinese in America," had flourished into a very active and important girls' club since January 5, 1931, the date of its first meeting at the International Institute. Most remembered for their elaborately themed carnivals, they also engaged in many social and volunteer activities. The Club's first aims were to "do our utmost to uphold the traditions of sportsmanship and to maintain friendship through our athletic, social, and philanthropic activities." On occasion, they competed with the Lowa girls in basketball and invited each other to social activities.

Under the faithful sponsorship of Maye Wong, the Mei Wah Club girls addressed a very important need for the Chinese American youth. In order to strengthen and make friends outside the family, school, and church, the girls initially occupied themselves with sporting events. The commitment and conviction of Wong provided the stability and direction that allowed the club to remain active through the war years. Wong recalls that the club was very family-oriented, and the girls frequently asked their sisters and cousins to join. Consequently, the club never really acquired new members outside the participating families, since the older members remained. In this way, the club's objectives changed as did the members' interests as they grew older.

The Mei Wah Club was active in many war relief efforts, organizing fund-raisers and participating in cultural events. Their performance at one event led to the formation of a drum corps, which, under the direction of David SooHoo, became very popular in the Southland. The drum corps attracted many members. Most of these girls averaged 16 years to 23 years in age, and met every week to practice in the parking lots of Chinatown. In 1939, the drum corps was invited to participate in the nationwide All Western Band Review at Long Beach, and they captured first place in their division. Surprised and thrilled at their achievement, they returned the following year, not only to gain for the second time the divisional award, but also the Sweepstakes trophy for scoring the most points over all the divisions of performing bands. Their last performance was at the opening dedication of the Chinese Consolidated Benevolent Association building located on 925 N. Broadway, on May 18, 1952. Many of the girls by that time had moved on, married, or taken on other interests.

By 1951, the year of their twentieth anniversary, many of the Mei Wah girls had grown into women. The club consequently took on a slightly different turn in its activities, shedding athletic activities for social and philanthropic activities. Since then, many club members, their daughters, and nieces have participated in these affairs, including the many festive and holiday gatherings, banquets, and dances. In the last 15 years, the Mei Wah Club has met once a month, planning one fund-raising project a year, with proceeds going towards scholarships.

The Mei Wah Club has recognized the balance between socializing and social conscience in their many contributions to the Chinese American and greater Los Angeles communities. In the past 50 years, they have supported such organizations as the Ming Sum School for Blind Orphan Girls in China; the Exceptional Children's Foundation and its teenage workshop; the American Indian Group; the Chung Wah Chinese School; the True

Light Presbyterian Church's library; the children's library at Castelar Elementary School; and Belmont, Marshall, and Lincoln High Schools by providing scholarships.

Kuan Ying Girls' Club. Kuan Ying Girls' Club was founded by Mabel Hong, to give young Chinese American women an opportunity to meet and socialize among themselves. Comprised of girls in their late teens and early twenties, their club was named after the Chinese woman folk hero and beautiful goddess, Kuan Ying.

In one aspect, the Kuan Ying Girls' Club was less active than the Mei Wah, whose activities were not only social, but philanthropic in scope. However, Kuan Ying served an equally important role for the girls who had become part of this short-lived club. Lilly Mu Lee was first involved in her late teens and remembers its members were mainly interested in forming a social club. The Kuan Ying club was most noted for their New Year's Eve dances, in which hundreds of young Chinese American men and women attended. The Club broke up as the girls grew older, some marrying and some moving away.

Lowa Auxiliary Girls' Club. Consisting of about 25 teenage to college-age girls who wanted to start their basketball team, this club was an auxiliary to the Lowa Boys' Club. Though the girls used the name of the Lowa, Elsie Wong remembered that there was no formal affiliation with Lowa Boys' Club. Instead, the Girls' Club was affiliated with the Girls' Reserve of the YWCA.

Formed in the mid-1930's, they competed against the Mei Wah girls' team, as well as other girls' teams around Los Angeles. Without a designated sponsor, they did have coaching assistance from other sports-minded young Chinese American women like Wong and were considered one of the best Chinese girls' basketball teams in Los Angeles. They practiced at Hazard Playground in East Los Angeles, 21st Street Playground, and later at Polytechnic High School.

The Lowa Auxiliary disbanded sometime after the end of World War II, when some girls soon took interests in other sports like bowling and tennis, while others moved onto other kinds of activities.

Cathayette Girls' Club. Like the Lowa Auxiliary, the Cathay-ettes was an athletic club without formal sponsorship. The Ca-thayettes, formed in the mid-1940's after the Lowa Girls' team disbanded, consisted primarily of young high school girls who attended the same elementary school (Castelar), the same high school (Belmont or Lincoln), the same Chinese school (at the Chinese Catholic Center), and the same church (the Chinese Catholic Center) in Chinatown.

Because they wanted to play basketball together on a regular basis, they formed the Cathayettes. Many of the members of the basketball team were from the Chinese Catholic Center, but it is uncertain whether or not they were sponsored by the Center. Considered the only Chinese girls' basketball team at the time, they played against other girls' teams around the area. Elsie Wong recalls that, "It was just something we enjoyed doing together." Other group activities included bowling and tennis. They also joined other social groups in taking turns sponsoring a record hop at local facilities in Boyle Heights and elsewhere in Los Angeles. The Cathayettes drew their activities to a close in the early 1950's, when most of the girls made their way onto college.

Chinese Drum and Bugle Corps (1954). Serving the youth of the community from ages 12 to 21, the first coed Chinese Drum and Bugle Corps of Los Angeles was started in 1954 by Bill Lee. Organized initially to assist the Chung Wah Chinese language school in fund-raising and recruitment efforts, the drum corps became an instant success and was quite popular among the many Chinese American youth in the community.

Practicing first at the Chung Wah School on Yale Street, the drum corps moved their practices to Nightingale Junior High. Many Chinese American women assumed important roles of lead-ership in the Corps, as well as provided assistance as chaperones and in the maintenance of uniforms. The drum corps grew in membership, and at one point peak to 250 young Chinese Ameri-cans in number. State-wide competitions brought many of the Chinese American youth together and offered them many op-portunities to travel. Sometimes, members even travelled across

the country. Their skill, precision, and prize-winning performances gave the Chinese American community in Los Angeles
much to be proud of.

The parents' auxiliary of the Drum Corps organized the largest
and most popular social event of the year, their fashion show
luncheon. All their fund-raising efforts went towards the maintenance and purchase of uniforms, instruments, music, and travel.
The Chinese Drum and Bugle Corps served the community for
nearly 25 years before disbanding, due to waning interest and
support within the community.

In Other Organizations

Other organizations developing in and around the perimeter
of the Chinese American community included both Chinese and
non-Chinese men and women.

China Society of Southern California (1935). The China
Society of Southern California was founded in 1935 by a group
of Chinese and non-Chinese and still exists today. Its primary purpose is to promote a true understanding and appreciation of the
history, culture, ideas, and customs of the Chinese people. Monthly meetings were and still are held in a Chinese restaurant. Programs in the past included speeches about Chinese culture and
history, Chinese music, dancing, drama, and sometimes films.
Scholarships have also been awarded to Chinese students who
pursued education in America.

In the past, the Chinese constituted no more than 20 percent
of the entire membership, but played an important role in the
Society. Many Chinese women not only participated in Society's
activities, but also took the leadership in many areas. Wen-Hui
Chen, who earned her doctorate degree in Sociology at USC, was
a frequent guest speaker on her study of Chinese Americans in
Los Angeles. Caroline Chan and Martha Chow were charter
members, board members, and guest speakers, and held official
positions for many years. In 1969, Bessie Loo became the first

Chinese woman to be elected as the president of the Society. Their active involvement in organizations such as the China Society reflects their tremendous leadership capabilities.

Ginling Alumni Association. Composed of those who either taught or studied at Ginling College in Nanking, China, the Ginling Alumni Association had both local and national chapters all over America. A very prestigious women's college, Ginling College was attended by many women who have since made their home in America. The alumni association has had as its past presidents Lily Ho Quon and Beulah Quo.

Chinatown Democratic Club (1958). Phoebe Yee and Dolores Wong were founding charter members and officers of this political organization which started in 1958. Working with Democratic candidates, the club contained many non-Chinese members and was active in political circles for many years.

In addition to political campaigning and fund-raising for a candidate, the Club has been instrumental in getting out the Democratic vote in Chinatown. Maintaining an average membership of about 50, the Club has also participated in county and state-wide Democratic conventions. The first woman taking leadership in the organization was Dolores Wong, the club's first vice-president.

Women honored for their pioneering achievements in building and enriching community by the Chinese Historical Society of Southern California in 1984. Left-to-right: Dr. Ruby Ling Louie, Beulah Quo, Mrs. She Wing SooHoo, Katherine Cheung, Barbara Jean Lee, and Ella Yee Quan.

Closing

The image of the passive, obedient and homebound Chinese woman is clearly contradicted by the lives of many of the pathbreakers described in this book. Chinese American women became journalists, waitresses, teachers, factory workers, actresses, and other workers. As pioneers, they often braved harsh, discriminatory working conditions and unfair employment practices. They also had to juggle the demands of work with their family responsibilities. The contributions of these Chinese women to their families, to the Chinese community, and to all of society were the result of long hours of labor and creative management of their time. Some of these women were forced into these active roles by economic necessity and historical circumstance, but others simply seized the opportunity to realize their potential. Initially rather homogeneous in regional culture, language and social backgrounds, Chinese American women became increasingly a heterogeneous group. Yet their shared ancestry and experiences of being a racial minority in America continued to bind them together. The strength and courage of these Chinese women in breaking barriers are an inspirational legacy to their daughters and granddaughters.

Appendices

Glossary

Beijing	北京
Canton	廣東（廣州）
cheong sam	長衫
Ching Ming	清明
Chung Wah school	中華學校
dim sum	點心
ERA	Equal Rights Amendment
fat choy	髮菜（發財）
Fujien	福建
Guangdong	廣東
Ginling Alumni Association	金陵大學校友會
Ginling College	金陵大學
Hakka	客家
Hok Sahn	鶴山
jaai	齋
joong	粽
Jung Jing Road	中正路
Kang Yuwei	康有為
Kong Chow Temple	岡州帝廟
Kuan Ti	關帝
Kuan Ying	觀音
Kuomintang	國民黨
Lowa	羅華
Loyola	Loyola-Marymount University
mahjong	麻將
Mei Wah	美華
moon-yuet	滿月
Nanking	南京
Punti	本地
Sa Hee	煞氣
Sam Yup	三邑
Sun Wui	新會
Sze Yup	四邑
USC	University of Southern California
Yi Go	二哥
Yi So	二嫂
YWCA	Young Women's Christian Association

Acknowledgments

We acknowledge the following Chinese American women of Southern California for sharing their experiences. Most of these persons were participants in the Southern California Chinese American Oral History Project.

Ethel Cannon
Caroline Chan
Lily Lum Chan
Mary Chan
Wen Hui Chung Chen
Katherine Cheung
Lai-Mun Ching
Ann H. Chinn
Elaine Chow
Grace Chow
Martha Chow
Ella Chung
Nellie Yee Chung
Noemi Crews
Marjorie Dong
Nancy Dennis
Ida Fong
Lena Fong
Lillian Fong
Kay Wong Gee
Oak Yip Gee
Margie Leong Hee
Alice Hom
Mabel Hong
Florence Hoy
Bessie Jeong
Alice Young Joe
Edith Q. Jung
Florence Haw Jung
Ying Wong Kwan
Rose Lamb
Louise Leung Larson
Barbara Jean Lee
Celia Y. F. Lee

Ida Lee
Lilly M. Lee
Margaret K. Lee
Betty Wong Lem
Bernice Leung
Lillie Lee Leung
Mabel Lum Lew
Bessie Loo
Lillie Louie
Marie Louie
Stella C. Louis
Chiung L. Lui
May Jung Lum
Soy Lung
Marge Ong
Beulah Quo
Him Gin Quon
Bernice Sam
Dorothy Siu
Rose Nim Tom
Jacqueline G. Ung
Louise Whiting
Clara Wong
Daisy Sui-Ying Wong
Dolores Wong
Elsie L. Wong
Jennie Lee Wong
Lillian Wong
May Wong
Maye Wong
Rose Wong
Ruth Kim Wong
Lim Kin Yee
Ora Yuen

We thank Judith Luther Wilder for preparing the dedication to Helen Lim Young, and Earl Wong for preparing the map graphic.

The many donors of the Helen Young Memorial Fund are gratefully acknowledged.

Photographs courtesy of

Asian American Studies Center, UCLA

California State University, Los Angeles

Wen Hui Chung Chen

Suellen Cheng

Katherine Cheung

Grace Chow

Fred Chung

Nellie Yee Chung

Hazel Kwok

Munson A. Kwok

Lilly Mu Lee

Mabel and George Lew

Bessie Loo

Los Angeles County Museum of Natural History

Ruby Ling Louie

Soy Lung

Marge and Oliver Ong

Henry S. Quan

Peter SooHoo, Jr.

Institutions

ASIAN AMERICAN STUDIES CENTER, UNIVERSITY OF CALIFORNIA, LOS ANGELES

The UCLA Asian American Studies Center was established in 1969 through the joint efforts of students and faculty to meet the needs of Asian Americans and to provide new perspectives and insights into Asian American culture, experiences and issues. The Center strives toward these goals by supporting research activities, curriculum, publications, a library collection, and student and community projects.

CHINESE HISTORICAL SOCIETY OF SOUTHERN CALIFORNIA

The Chinese Historical Society of Southern California is dedicated to 1) bringing together people with a common interest in the history of Chinese in Southern California, and 2) promoting a better understanding of the Chinese American heritage in relation to American society. Major functions include supporting and conducting research, collecting materials and artifacts, disseminating historical information, stimulating interest in Chinese American history, and working in historical preservation and cooperating with other societies for the broader historical perspective. The Society is a non-profit corporation.

BOARD OF DIRECTORS, 1984
Munson Kwok, President
Evelyn Cucchiarella,
  Vice President
Mary Yee, Secretary
Ella Y. Quan, Treasurer
Kaza Q. Dong,
  Membership Secretary

Marion Fay (Jan. to June)
Elmo Gambarana
Donald Loo
Albert Lum
George Morris
Eugene W. Moy (June to Dec.)

BOOK COMMITTEE
Ella Y. Quan, Chairperson
Marion Fay
Munson Kwok
Chong Lew
Donald Loo

Eugene Wong Moy
Gerald Shue
Angela Ma Wong
Art Young

BOOK PRODUCTION COMMITTEE
Ella Y. Quan, Chairperson
Suellen Cheng
Elmo Gambarana
Munson Kwok
Russell Leong
Margie Lew

Linda Lum
Eugene W. Moy
Susan Sing
Angela Ma Wong
Earl Wong

NOTES